STORM
PROOF
YOUR
MONEY

STORM PROOF YOUR MONEY

WEATHER ANY ECONOMY,
REBUILD YOUR PORTFOLIO,
PROTECT YOUR FUTURE

Brett Arends

WILEY

John Wiley & Sons, Inc.

Published by John Wiley & Sons, Inc., Hoboken, New Jersey.
Published simultaneously in Canada.

For general information on our other products and services or for technical
support, please contact our Customer Care Department within the United States at
(800) 762-2974, outside the United States at (317) 572-3993 or fax (317) 572-4002.

Wiley also publishes its books in a variety of electronic formats. Some content that
appears in print may not be available in electronic books. For more information
about Wiley products, visit our web site at www.wiley.com.

Library of Congress Cataloging-in-Publication Data:
Arends, Brett.
     Storm proof your money : weather any economy, rebuild your portfolio,
protect your future / Brett Arends.
          p. cm.
     Includes index.
       ISBN 978-0-470-48268-1 (hardback)
     1. Finance, Personal. 2. Investments. I. Title.
     HG179.A67 2009
     332.6—dc22

                                                              2009029133

Printed in the United States of America.
10 9 8 7 6 5 4 3 2 1

For Linda

Contents

Acknowledgments   **xi**

Chapter 1   Getting Started   **1**
About Me   3
About This Book   3

Chapter 2   Checking the Map   **7**
The Lesson of Harry Patch   8
Santa Claus Isn't Coming to Town   9
Where Are You Trying to Go?   12
Where Are You Now?   16
How Much Do You Need to Save?   19
How Can You Move the Numbers in Your Favor?   23
Conclusion   28

Chapter 3   The Basics   **31**
Break Out of Debt   31
Secure Your Financial Lifelines   36
Check Your Big Risks   42
Conclusion   45

Chapter 4   How Not to Invest   **47**
Putting Too Much Faith in Stocks   48
Putting Too Much Faith in Phony Diversification   53
Taking Too Much Risk   55
Misunderstanding Your Mutual Funds   58

Chasing Performance   63
Trying to Find the Next Apple   65
Owning Shares in Your Employer   67
Keeping All Your Money in the Bank   69
Keeping All Your Money in Bonds   71
Stockpiling Gold   73
Investing Too Much in Real Estate   76
Conclusion   80

Chapter 5   Storm Proof Your Portfolio   83
Inflation-Protected Government Bonds   84
Global Index Funds   87
Flexible Funds   93
Covered Call Funds   106
Precious Metals   108
Taxable Bonds   112
Municipals   116
Closed-End Funds   118
Timing: Little and Often   120
How to Handle a Crash   123
Using Options for Financial Insurance   126
Conclusion   127

Chapter 6   Cash Flow Positive from Right Now   129
Your Hidden Costs   130
Repeat Costs   132
Give Yourself a Raise   135
How to Make $500,000 the Easy Way   138
Adding It All Up   155
Further Thoughts   156
Conclusion   158

Chapter 7   Cover Your Assets   161
Why Tax Shelters Are More Important Than Ever   161
Make the Most of Your 401(k)   164
Make the Most of Your IRA   165
Life Insurance and Variable Annuities   166
Self-Employed Shelters   168

Shelters and College Savings   168
Make the Most of Your Investment Losses   171
How Not to Lose Everything   173
Conclusion   175

Chapter 8   Next Steps   **177**
Checking the Map   177
The Basics   178
How Not to Invest   178
Storm Proof Your Portfolio   179
Cash Flow Positive from Right Now   179
Cover Your Assets   180
The Principles of Storm Proofing   180
Staying on Track   182
Getting Started   183

Appendix   Investment Spotlight   **185**

Index   **203**

Acknowledgments

This book took a few months to write but many years to develop. So many helped along the way. In my life I've learned almost as much from the wisdom of others as I have from my own mistakes.

In the world of finance, I am blessed to be able to count so many good and wise minds on both sides of the Atlantic among my friends. To all those who have helped shape my understanding—many thanks to Lloyd Glazer, Crispin Odey, Peter Bennett, Steve Russell, Joseph Nehorai, Andrew "Jocky" Roberts, Manu Daftary, Chuck Clough, David Bowers, Guy Feld, Hugh Young, James Montier, Karl "Chip" Case, Matt Patsky, Shigeki "Shag" Makino, Burr Clark, Bruce Eshbaugh, Bijal Shah, and Dan Bunting.

My career really began at McKinsey & Company, and I owe a big thank you to all my former colleagues—including Andrjez Klesyk, Andrew Doman, Julian Seaward, Paul McNamara, Jeff Luhnow, Felix Rubel, Hani Habbas, Demetrios Zoppos, and Vicki Harris. Thanks, also, to professors Philip Parker and Pekka Hietala at INSEAD, who first revealed to me the internal workings of the marketing industry and corporate finance.

I could never forget all the wonderful journalists I've worked with over the years, including Ruth Sunderland, Geoffrey Foster, Cliff Feltham, Michael Baws, Lucy Farndon, Tim Freeborn, Geoff Levy, Jerry Kronenberg, Jennifer Heldt Powell, David Morrow, Almar Latour, Alan Murray, Jason Zweig, Simon Constable, and Adam Najberg. Good colleagues and good friends—thank you all.

My many friends who have helped me, supported me, and encouraged me in so many ways—my deepest thanks to Mike Adam, Nick Thomas, Brenlen Jinkens, James Bullock, Adam Spielman, Carl Newns, Lewis Cutillo, Dave Taylor, James Hadley, Tip and Patricia Thiboutot, Fiona Henderson, George Gilpatrick,

Matt Black, Mark Waldron, Gillian Wilson, and Margaret Doyle. And a special thanks to Mark Hollak and Jan Dahlin Geiger for their helpful suggestions on the manuscript.

My editors—where would I have been without you? Neal Templin, Nikki Waller, Cybele Weisser, and Darren McDermott at the *Wall Street Journal*; Dave Callaway and Angela Moore at MarketWatch; Alison Coulter and Brian Cronk at TheStreet.com; Michael Walters, Brian O'Connor, and Alex Brummer at the *Daily Mail*; Cosmo Macero, Greg Gatlin, and Eric Convey at the *Boston Herald*; Duncan Campbell-Smith at the *Economist*; and Ra Tickel at the London *Daily Telegraph*. And thanks to Jay Mandel at William Morris, and Pamela van Giessen, Emilie Herman, Kate Wood, and Mary Daniello at John Wiley & Sons for making this book possible.

A very special mention to Andrew Alexander, who gave me vital help and guidance when I began my career in journalism. And my deepest thanks and love to my wonderful family, including my Mom, Andrew, Frances, Karen, Kirsten, and Richard. And above all to Linda, for everything.

Brett Arends

STORM PROOF YOUR MONEY

CHAPTER 1

Getting Started

If you are nervous of the stock market right now, no wonder. After recent events, many investors are feeling shocked and confused. Wall Street has plunged twice in a decade. (See Figure 1.1.) Those who hung on for dear life through the turmoil are wondering if they should get out. Those who bailed are asking when, if ever, it will be safe to get back in.

But if you don't invest in the stock market, where should you keep your money? How can you rebuild your nest egg and get back on track? And where does this leave your long-term plans? Can you still retire in comfort? If so, how?

If you are grappling with these questions, this book is for you.

I write an online personal finance column for the *Wall Street Journal.* When the crisis hit in September 2008 I was suddenly swamped with desperate e-mails from readers around the country, and around the world, asking more basic questions. Was the economy collapsing? What had just happened to their life savings? Was their retirement nest egg safe? Would they ever be able to send their children to college?

I was dismayed to discover how badly prepared so many people were—and, in many cases, how badly advised.

I heard from people in their seventies who had all their money in five stocks.

Figure 1.1 Standard & Poor's 500 Index, December 1996 to June 2009
Source: S&P Indexes.

And from those near retirement whose advisers had put their money into supposedly safe Fannie Mae and Freddie Mac preferred stock. (Value today: $0.)

And from those who had just lost a fortune on their own employer's stock. And from those horrified to discover their so-called diversification strategy consisted of five mutual funds invested in the stock market.

During the depths of the turmoil in 2008 and 2009, many investors couldn't withstand the losses and bailed—often right near the market lows. (That always happens.)

Far too much of the financial advice being doled out these days is painfully simplistic. There lots of books about "how to get rich" or "how to be rich." For most people, the more important issue is "how not to get poor." That's why I have written this book. The aim is to offer some help and guidance to get you back on track. It does not, obviously, replace a comprehensive financial plan. But it may help you understand what went wrong with your finances, why it went wrong, and what you can do about it.

The aim throughout is to offer practical, oven-ready tools you can apply to your own life. And it's written for everybody. I avoid jargon, roundabout speaking, and unneeded complexity. It doesn't assume you know much about the financial markets. As Albert

Einstein said, one should try to make things as simple as possible, but no simpler.

About Me

I have been working as a financial journalist, in Europe and here in the United States, since the 1990s. I began my career with McKinsey & Company, the strategic business consultancy. I was educated at Cambridge and Oxford Universities, and I have the Chartered Financial Consultant (ChFC) and Accredited Asset Management Specialist (AAMS) designations. My columns for TheStreet.com received an award from the Society of American Business Editors and Writers in 2008. I have been writing for the *Wall Street Journal* since 2007.

I never really trust somebody until I've heard them say two things: "I don't know" and "I was wrong." So let me say both here. I don't know what's going to happen next in the markets. Shares may boom or they may not. Inflation may take off or it may not. All sorts of things may happen. I don't know the future, and neither does anybody else. That's the reason for storm proofing your portfolio— so you don't need to know.

As for "I was wrong": Although it's true I wrote a number of columns before the financial crisis warning about the dangers, I didn't predict a crash as spectacular as the one we had. I wasn't anywhere near bearish enough.

Some of this book will sound critical of money managers and financial advisers. I should make it clear right here that this is not a blanket condemnation. There are many excellent managers and advisers out there doing a great job for their clients. I've spoken to plenty of them in the course of my work. As in any industry, some of the practitioners are high-caliber and some aren't.

About This Book

This book will take you through a series of steps addressing each aspect of your financial rebuilding plan.

It starts with Chapter 2 (Checking the Map). When it comes to their money, many people haven't even asked the most fundamental questions. Where are you going? How do you plan to get there? They have little idea how much they will actually need in order to retire in comfort, or to send the children to college. Many aren't even sure how to go about finding the answer, either. And no one seems to want to tell them, clearly and simply. This chapter addresses that need. It is designed to help you take charge of your financial situation.

We'll start by looking at the scale of the problem: How and why so many people are so financially unprepared. Then we'll look at the basic tools you need to draw up your own financial road map. The focus here is on keeping things as straightforward as possible. It will help you calculate how much you will likely need to retire or send your children to college, what sort of investment returns you can rely on to help you get there, and how much you will need to save.

Some of these answers may look alarming. Too many people, alas, have been told the road is much easier than it is. But the chapter will conclude with some other strategies to help you get to your destination.

Chapter 3 (The Basics) covers three basic steps toward strengthening your financial position: paying off your credit cards, securing your emergency lifelines, and making sure you have the insurance coverage you need.

If you are struggling under credit card debt, I'll explain why paying that off is the most powerful first financial move you can make. And we'll look at some tips and traps for doing that as fast as possible.

The second key move is to secure your emergency lifelines. In this turbulent economy, families need to have emergency reserves they can tap at short notice if economic trouble hits. Many commentators will advise you to keep large amounts of cash in a bank account. I'll explain the hidden dangers in that approach, and alternatives that will serve you better.

Third, we'll look briefly at insurance, and the importance of making sure your major risks are covered. It's easy to focus on other areas of your financial situation, only to get blindsided by sudden events.

Chapter 4 (How Not to Invest) takes a look at the investment challenge ahead of you. It may seem odd to start by talking about what *not* to do. But successful investing is like driving: Most of the battle lies in staying on the road and avoiding accidents. In this chapter we'll walk through the investment landscape and look at why so many investors end up in the ditch.

Few financial topics are as misunderstood as investing. For all those trying in vain to win the jackpot through desperate speculation, there are many others sitting on the sidelines because they find the markets too dangerous, or simply incomprehensible.

Some of my points may sound surprising. That's because they go against a lot of conventional wisdom. Many investors have been fooled into believing they could rely on pat investment rules and cheap nostrums to reach their goals. These ideas have been peddled by what I call the "McMoney" wing of the finance industry. They're a big reason so many people face such problems today.

Chapter 5 (Storm Proof Your Portfolio) then looks at how to tackle your investment challenges. We'll consider how to build a new kind of investment portfolio that can weather all seasons. Too many people worry about what the markets are going to do next month, or next year. The challenge is to arrange your finances as far as possible so you don't have to care. We'll look at a range of options that can help you build a portfolio that is better protected against the elements. Finally, we'll look at other issues important to ordinary investors: how to ease yourself back into the markets, and how to handle a market crash.

The only way to build your financial security is to become cash flow positive. And that means to stop burning cash, and start earning it. That's the subject of Chapter 6 (Cash Flow Positive from Right Now). To have more money, you need to save more; and to save more, you need to spend less. You'd think that statement was a banality, wouldn't you? Instead, remarkably, a lot of people consider it controversial. So many people still desperately cling to the hope that they can save more without spending less, just as some people still hope to find a diet that lets them lose weight while eating lots of chocolate cake.

Like a battle between gluttons and anorexics, the debate over spending is in danger of being drawn to the two extremes: We're apparently either on the Home Shopping Network buying gold Homer Simpson dolls or we're supposed to be making new clothes out of lint.

The good news is that there is a happy medium. Spending less doesn't mean living like a pauper. It's about applying smart strategies. We'll look at some of the major hidden costs burning a hole in most families' budgets, and how to beat them. We'll then go through the typical spending areas of a middle-class family, and see how anyone can turn themselves cash flow positive without serious sacrifice, and start building wealth.

In these times we need all the help we can get, and that's the topic of Chapter 7 (Cover Your Assets). We'll look at some of the major breaks, loopholes, and shelters available to you, and see how to use them to maximum advantage to build your wealth and security. It's easy to overlook these breaks, especially in times of financial turbulence. But it's a mistake. Contrary to what some might tell you, these breaks are more important in a rocky economy than they are in a boom.

Finally, Chapter 8 (Next Steps) looks ahead at how to start putting this plan into effect in your life. It recaps the basic steps to planning for a retirement, a strategy for rebuilding your investment portfolio, plans to boost your savings and to make the most of your loopholes and shelters, and thoughts on how to make sure you stay on track.

CHAPTER 2

Checking the Map

When you get off track, it makes sense to pull over and check the map (or, this days, fiddle with the GPS). That's true if you're trying to get to Tallahassee for Thanksgiving, and it's true if you are trying to reach financial targets.

It's especially useful if you think you might be lost.

How much do you actually require to send the children to college, or to save for retirement? Where are you now? And how can you get from here to there? When it comes to retirement, every office has at least one Watercooler Guy who scares everybody by saying Social Security "won't be there when you retire" and tosses out terrifying numbers. "You need to have at least $2 million when you retire, or you're going to be living on cat food," he'll say, and nod sagely. (Watercooler Guy, of course, also has a 100 percent record of predicting World Series winners—in hindsight.)

Ignore him. Alas, many people in the money business aren't much help, either. Some of them will try to blind you with science. Others will intimidate you with crazy numbers plucked from thin air. Others, equally maddeningly, will answer the question with a string of questions of their own. "What sort of retirement do you want?" they'll ask. "What are your life goals? What is your risk tolerance?"

It's like the person who answers every question with the words "It depends."

On what? "That, too, depends."

Many people give up. They either stick their heads in the sand and ignore the subject, or they panic, or they figure they will put it off to another moment (and then they forget about it).

This chapter aims to cut through a lot of the noise. It should help you get a better idea of where you need to go and how to get there. It does not replace a full and comprehensive financial plan. Instead it covers the following points:

- Why so many Americans face a savings crisis.
- What you will need in order to retire comfortably (or— another important goal—to send the children to college).
- How much you should start saving now in order to reach your destination.
- What else you can do to help your plans.

The Lesson of Harry Patch

Harry Patch died in July 2009.

He was an ordinary Englishman, and lived an ordinary life in many ways. But there was one remarkable detail. Harry was one of the last surviving veterans of the First World War, which had ended 91 years earlier, in 1918.

Mr. Patch was born in 1898, and was 111 when he died. Henry Allingham, his fellow veteran, had died a week earlier at age 113.

Think of all that they saw during their lives. When they were born, Queen Victoria was the Empress of India and the British Navy ruled the waves. Guglielmo Marconi had not yet made his first radio broadcast. The Wright Brothers had not yet taken to the air.

They were already middle-aged by the time of the first atomic bomb and in their seventies when Neil Armstrong walked on the moon. When the Berlin Wall came down, Henry Allingham was 93.

If the past 100 years seems like a long time, look ahead. More and more of us can expect to live similar lengths of time. A full span of years is now much longer than three score and 10. Those reaching age 65 in good health should expect to live well into their eighties or longer. Many will live a full century.

This means people are likely to spend much more time in retirement than they anticipate. Retirement, once a coda to your productive years, is now a genuine third stage of life.

Living it well will cost a lot of money. So, too, will living it in dignity and comfort when your health deteriorates. A private room in a nursing home now costs an average of $77,000 a year. An assisted living facility costs $36,000. Home health aides cost around $20 an hour or more. Costs of medical care and assistance have been rising faster than inflation for a long time, and there is no reason to think they will start getting cheaper. On the contrary, this rise in costs is imposing a greater and greater strain on the finances of senior citizens and their families.

It's much more expensive to grow old than it used to be.

But most people are unprepared.

Today, two-thirds of American workers have set aside less than $50,000 for their retirement. That dismal information comes from a 2009 survey by the Employee Benefit Research Institute, a leading think tank specializing in retirement issues. To put this in context, $50,000 in savings is going to generate retirement income of maybe $200 a month. Forty percent of American workers have saved less than $10,000 for retirement.

Of course this includes a fair number of young workers who have years left to build up their savings. But it also includes a lot of older workers nearing retirement as well, including many of the baby boom generation.

The picture is even worse among those who have already retired. Fifty-six percent of retirees have less than $25,000 set aside.

How are they going to support themselves into their eighties or nineties? What are they going to live on?

Santa Claus Isn't Coming to Town

In the case of many, they're relying on the Santa Claus retirement plan. It has two simple steps:

1. Save nothing.
2. Hope Santa shows up with a big sack of money before they turn 65.

It's been a popular plan—the most popular in the country.

Back in the 1990s a lot of people thought Santa had arrived on Wall Street. It is amazing to think how many genuinely assumed that the stock market would allow them to double their money every few years with no real risk or effort. No wonder the savings rate collapsed. With Santa on his way, who needed to save? All you needed was an index fund. Riches for all!

Then it was the dot-com bubble. You just had to keep buying Yahoo!, or Cisco Systems, or Pets.com. That NASDAQ commercial they used to show during football games ("the stock market for the next 100 years"), with its inexorably rising chart line, seemed to point the way to easy wealth.

When that dream ended, as dreams are apt to do, millions turned their hopes to something else: their homes. By 2004 the same people who had thought shares were going to double every few years now believed their homes were going to pull off the same trick.

Those were extraordinary times. Millions got used to them and thought they were normal.

In September 1999, a new book boldly predicted the Dow Jones Industrial Average was heading for 36,000. At the time the Dow was just below 11,000. Almost exactly 10 years later, when this manuscript was being finished, it was a little over 9,000. Even when you include reinvested dividends, the total return on the U.S. stock market over that time was minuscule. And when you adjust for inflation, investors lost about one-fifth of their money.

As for houses: When you look beyond the immediate crisis, the underlying picture isn't interesting. It's dull. We have just lived through the biggest house price boom and bust in American history. The net result? By early 2009 American homeowners who had held their homes for 15 years had made only about 2.5 percent a year more than inflation. Over 20 years it was barely 1 percent.

And that's the real message of the past 10 years. It isn't that the Dow is going to zero. It's that it *isn't* going to 36,000. And homes aren't worthless—they just aren't, in many cases, going to make you rich enough to retire on.

Sorry, folks. Santa Claus isn't coming to town.

Meanwhile, many American households have been getting into poor financial shape.

Figure 2.1, from the United States Bureau of Economic Analysis, shows the national savings rate. By 2005 the average household was saving as little as families did in the depths of the Great Depression.

The second picture is even worse. Figure 2.2 comes from data tracked by the Federal Reserve. It shows household debts in relation to incomes. While the typical family has saved less and less, it has borrowed more and more.

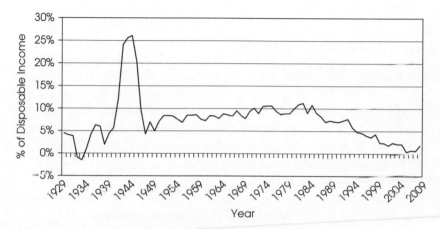

Figure 2.1   U.S. Savings Rate from 1928 to 2009

Source: United States Bureau of Economic Analysis.

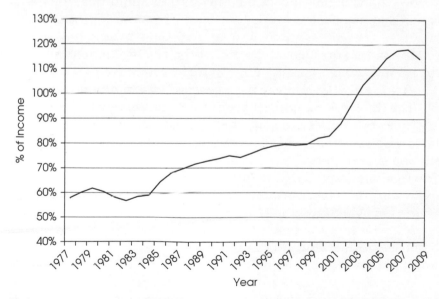

Figure 2.2   U.S. Household Debts as a Percentage of Personal Income, 1977 to 2009

Source: Federal Reserve.

Back in the age of Santa Claus—Dow heading for 36,000 and all that—this didn't seem to matter. Everyone assumed their assets would keep rising magically to offset the value of the debt. But it matters now. It makes saving for retirement an even bigger challenge for many people.

Where Are You Trying to Go?

Planning your financial future isn't that different from planning a trip.

Choose your destination. Check where you are now. Then work backwards from your destination to find the route.

How does this work in practice? You should start by choosing your destination. If you are planning for your retirement, this is a three-step process.

1. Estimate the income you'll need when you're retired.
2. Calculate how much you'll have to provide from your own savings.
3. Calculate how much you'll need to save in order to generate that income each year.

I've put a worksheet at the end of the chapter to help you track the numbers. Let's take each one in turn.

Step 1: Estimate the income you'll need when you're retired.

The full-service approach is to sit down with a financial planner and work out a plan in detail. That can include drawing up budgets for everything from living expenses and health care costs to travel, shopping, and other discretionary expenses.

That's the approach recommended by Jan Dahlin Geiger, an experienced financial planner and the author of *Get Your Assets in Gear!* (Outskirts Press, 2007). It's what she's always done with her clients. And this is a good idea if you can work with a high-quality financial planner. But it's complex. You're not going to do it right now. And you may put it off for a lot longer.

According to a survey by the Employee Benefit Research Institute, fewer than half of working-age people have even tried to calculate what they will need to retire comfortably.

Furthermore, as Daniel Gilbert points out in *Stumbling on Happiness* (Random House, 2006), human beings are often pretty poor at imagining what will make them happy in the future.

Here's the self-service option. If you want to estimate the disposable income you are likely to need in retirement, the best place to start is by looking at the disposable income you have now.

You already have good experience of the standard of living this provides.

Your disposable income, of course, isn't the same as your gross income.

When you're retired, you won't be paying payroll taxes. You'll also be spared some other work-related costs, like commuting.

You won't have to save for your retirement, of course.

It's usually a good idea to pay off your mortgage by the time you retire, if you can. And if you do that, then of course that's another cost you won't have.

Many people argue that, as a rough rule of thumb, you will probably only need about 75 percent of your current gross income to maintain the same standard of living. Depending on the size of your mortgage, and other expenses, it may be more or less.

There are plenty of caveats to bear in mind. People who want to spend their golden years traveling the world in style are going to need a lot more than someone who wants to sit in a small town and paint pictures of the mountains.

Whatever figure you settle on, you now have the first key element of your plan. This is your target retirement income. That's the first line of the retirement planning worksheet at the end of this chapter.

Step 2: Calculate how much you'll have to provide from your own savings.

Some of your target income, of course, will come from Social Security and any other pension benefits you can expect. For most middle-class people, Social Security is and will probably remain a core part of their retirement plan.

To find out how much you can expect in benefits, the Social Security Administration offers online calculators. You can find them at www.socialsecurity.gov/planners/calculators.htm and www.socialsecurity.gov/estimator/. The average benefit in 2009 was about $14,000 for a retired individual and $22,500 for a couple. The Social Security Administration says it aims to provide about 40 percent of preretirement income for the average retiree.

There is, of course, a lot of debate about Social Security's future. Plenty of doomsayers are predicting its demise. But such statements are almost certainly a wild exaggeration.

Yes, the system faces financial pressures. People are living longer. The enormous baby boom generation is just starting to retire, and they will sharply increase the costs. So the system is going to have to adapt.

But the changes needed to rebalance it aren't as drastic as some suggest. The minimum retirement age may rise a bit. So may payroll taxes. Benefits may get shaved. There's no doubt this will put more pressure on future retirees. You need to be better prepared than previous generations. But Social Security should still be there.

A diminishing number of people can also rely on a traditional pension as well. If that includes you, contact the provider and find out what your pension income is likely to be each month. Add that to the Social Security payments you expect.

You now know your likely Social Security and pension income. That's the second line of the retirement planning worksheet.

Obviously the income you won't get from these you will need to provide from your own sources. That's your retirement income gap.

If you want $70,000 a year in retirement, and you can expect only $20,000 from Social Security and your pension, you are going to need to supply the extra $50,000 yourself. If you want a retirement income of $50,000 and Social Security will provide just $25,000, you will need to generate an extra $25,000 a year.

This retirement income gap, meaning the extra income you will need to generate from your own sources, goes on the third line of the retirement planning worksheet.

Step 3: Calculate how much you'll need to save in order to generate that income each year.

It's a reasonable assumption that, once you are retired, your savings should be able to earn at least 3 percent a year more than inflation even if the money is invested conservatively. Caution: It's not guaranteed. But it's a deliberately conservative estimate. Some, still living in the age of Santa Claus, may think that's too low. And perhaps it is. But that's the only safe way to plan: using conservative assumptions.

If you retire at around 65, you should also plan to make your money last another 30 to 35 years. Most people won't live that long, of course. But you have to draw the line somewhere. Once again, you need to plan conservatively. You are far better having your money outlast you than the reverse.

Using these two assumptions, the retirement math follows simply.

For each $1 a year of retirement income that you need to generate, you will probably need to save about $20 by the time you retire. Call it the Rule of 20.

So if you need to generate retirement income of $10,000 a year from your savings, you will need to save about $200,000 by age 65. If you want $50,000 a year, you will need to save about $1 million. And so on.

In the retirement planning worksheet, multiply the third line by 20. That gives your savings target. This is a key number and is the fourth line in the retirement planning worksheet.

You now have some idea of how much you are likely to need in order to retire in comfort.

An illustration: Let's say you figure you will need 75 percent of your preretirement income to maintain the same standard of living after you retire. And the Social Security Administration says it aims to provide 40 percent of that. If those numbers apply to you, you're going to need to find another 35 percent of your current income from your own savings. The Rule of 20 says that in that case your savings target would be about seven times your preretirement income (or 20 times 35 percent).

For most people, this would probably be a lowball figure. Higher-income earners, in particular, will probably find that Social Security won't produce anywhere near 40 percent of their current income. They may find they need to save nine or 10 times their current income as a result.

You may have seen advertisements by insurance companies offering annuity rates of 5 percent or 6 percent. But you have to be careful. Those advertised figures are usually in *nominal* returns. In other words, they take no account of inflation. That's just a money illusion. If you lock in a return of 6 percent and then prices start rising by 8 percent a year, you are going to go backwards. What really matters is your *real* rate of return—in other words, the amount you earn on top of inflation. If you want to maintain a standard of living, that's what counts. Throughout this book I will use real rates of return in my calculations. Real, postinflation rates are the only way to make meaningful calculations.

(Of course you can use your own, different assumptions. If your investments manage to beat inflation by 5 percent a year and you only want them to last 30 years, you would need only about 15 times your annual income target. In contrast, if you are very conservative and figure you might beat inflation by only about 2 percent, you would need to save about 25 times your annual income.)

The math for other long-term financial goals follows the same principles.

Saving for college? You know how long you have: If the child is a newborn, you have about 18 years. The earlier you start saving, the better.

As of 2009, tuition and fees for in-state students at a public university average about $6,600 a year, while those at a private university average about $25,000.* Add in typical room, board, and basic living expenses, and a year at State U costs about $14,300 while a year at the average private college comes to $34,000.

But that's only half the story. Grants and federal tax benefits will often kick in a good chunk of that. The net result, according to the College Board: The typical student at State U needs to find about $10,600 a year, and a student at a private college about $24,000. For four years that's $42,400 at State U, $96,000 private.

Where will these costs be in 18 years' time, when your child is ready to start his or her freshman year?

Nobody knows, of course. Over the past 15 years these net college costs have risen about 2 percentage points a year faster than inflation. That may not continue; prices of things rarely rise faster than general inflation indefinitely.

But if it does continue, in 18 years those costs will be about 43 percent higher than today in real terms. That means $61,000 in today's money for four years at State U, and $137,000 at a private college.

Where Are You Now?

Now that you have some idea of where you want to go, it's time to look at where you are starting from.

How much have you saved already?

---

*College Board, *Trends in College Pricing*, 2008–2009.

College Costs

- Four years in-state at State University costs the average student $42,400 in tuition and living expenses, net of average aid.
- At a private college the average is more than twice as much, or $96,000.

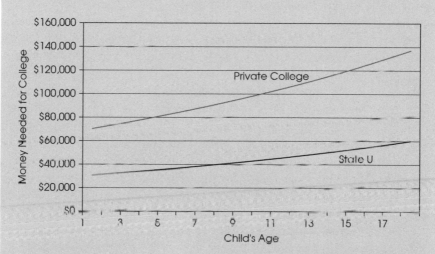

A simple illustration of the challenge many American families face in trying to save up to send children to college. If recent trends continue—a big if, admittedly—then by the time they turn 18 children born today will need to have about $60,000, in today's dollars, to go to their state's public university. They will need almost $140,000 to go to the average private college. The lines show where the college savings accounts would need to be, at each birthday, in order to need no further contributions. (The chart assumes college prices rise by 2 percent faster than inflation each year, while the investments earn 4 percent.)

If college costs keep rising at recent rates, a child born today will need:

- $61,000 in 18 years' time to go to the State University.
- $137,000 to go to a typical private college.

Okay, this amount probably isn't what it was a few years ago. But no cheating. Historical cost doesn't count. Your shares are worth only what the market will pay today. Same for that investment property in Orlando.

Many people respond to financial turmoil with various forms of denial or dubious mental accounting. They may not open the envelopes from the brokerage firm. When markets fall they say they will "wait until things recover" before they reevaluate their investments. They pretend their home or their investments are actually worth their peak values.

But if you really want to get an honest picture of where you stand, you need to see the present through clear eyes. That means looking at what investments are worth today.

Add up all your investments. That includes any savings in 401(k) or equivalent plans, like a 403(b). It includes any individual retirement accounts (IRAs). It includes any other investments and any money in savings or other bank accounts. No, it doesn't matter what your investments were worth last year or at the peak or even last month. What are they worth *today*?

Then subtract any debts. That includes any student loans, car loans, and credit card debt.

That gives you a figure for your net worth. It goes on the fifth line of the worksheet.

In the previous section, you worked out where you were going: your retirement savings target.

Now you also know where you're starting from. Obviously the distance you still need to travel is the distance between the two, your savings gap. In the worksheet at the end of the chapter, this goes on the sixth line.

(Write the total, representing your current net worth, in line five of the retirement planning worksheet. Now subtract this number from line four, which is the amount you need to save by the time you are 65. The difference is your savings gap—the distance you still need to cover. Write that on line six.)

Home equity is part of your savings. For many people it's the most important part. Some advisers say you shouldn't count this because they figure your home isn't going to generate income in retirement. But the right to live in your home is a form of income.

After all, if you don't need to spend $20,000 a year on accommodation once you retire, then you won't need to earn $20,000, net of tax, to pay for it, either.

The important thing is to count your home equity once, but *only* once.

So if you are paying off a mortgage and you expect to have paid it off in full by the time you retire, then you can either include your home equity in your net worth or exclude your accommodation costs from your retirement income needs.

You can, of course, convert your home equity into liquid savings when you retire if you need to. You could sell your home, invest or save the proceeds, and use the interest on the savings to pay rent on somewhere else. Or you could take out a reverse mortgage. That's a process that converts home equity into a type of annuity, letting you live in your home for life and providing you with an income stream. It's not for everyone. Among the issues is the fact that the fees can be extremely high. It may only be worth considering as a last resort. But it's an option.

How Much Do You Need to Save?

Now you have a better idea of the distance you still have to cover to reach your goal. That's your savings gap. So how do you get there?

We've already seen that far too many people have been relying on the Santa Claus savings plan. The idea was that they didn't have to save very much because the stock market or their home value was going to do all the work for them.

Many believed, or were sold, the fanciful idea that the stock market goes up about 10 percent a year. But it's an unreliable number—and another example of a money illusion. It takes no account for inflation. The real or after-inflation returns have been much lower.

Before the 2008 crash, when I commented in the *Wall Street Journal* on the low national savings rate, a number of readers wrote in to disagree. American households, they assured me, had no need to sock away a lot more money. They were building up their wealth automatically through their booming home values and stock market accounts.

Another dangerous idea is that investors can control their long-term returns simply by taking on more risk or volatility. So, according to this theory, if you want to end up with more you don't really need to save more. You just have to ratchet up your risk levels and invest more aggressively.

This is why so many people were pouring money into small company stocks and certain overseas markets at exactly the wrong moment.

It is nowhere near being that simple.

Many of the most successful investors in history—most famously Warren Buffett, the world's second-richest man—have actually followed a policy of avoiding excessive risks. It is a Hollywood-type myth that investors make their money by throwing double sixes. It frequently ends in tears.

You cannot control your returns so closely. Your money will be at the mercy of the markets.

No one knows exactly how investments will do over the next 10 or 20 years. If shares match historic returns, they may earn 5 or 6 percent above inflation. But of course that's uncertain. And markets are volatile. You may hope for the best, but you need to plan for the worst.

This is a critical issue. It's the reason so many are in financial trouble today. They built their plans based on assumptions that were only best guesses. The issue isn't where your retirement plans will be if markets boom over the next 20 years. It's where they will be if markets don't.

For many of my estimates in this book I've used more modest forecasts for investment returns. I've assumed that investors may earn around 4.5 percent a year in real, postinflation terms. That's a reasonably low estimate. And it's okay for certain forecasts. But for the sake of planning I'd err even a little more on the side of caution. So in this chapter, when it comes to making plans, I've set the numbers at around 4 percent. That's a sensible move. Remember there are absolutely no guarantees. The results could come in even lower. Any forecast about the future is going to be a guess, based on history and logic. At least this is a conservative one.

If you make longer-term plans based on that, you are unlikely to end up substantially disappointed. And if market returns come in much better than expected and you end up with too much money, well, you'll just have to sue me.

Now the road map to your destination becomes clearer.

Saving for retirement? Earlier in this chapter you calculated how much you will need to save by the time you turn 65. You then worked out how much you have so far. The difference, obviously, is the gap you need to close. Now you know what sort of returns you can hope for.

So how much will you need to save each year, between now and your retirement, to reach your goal?

Table 2.1 runs the numbers. Based on investment returns of 4 percent real per year, it shows the amount, rounded to the nearest $100, you'd need to save each year to reach these targets by age 65.

Based on these assumptions, someone who is 30 years old who wants to save another $250,000 before retiring should look at saving $3,100 a year to get there. Someone who is 45 and hopes to accumulate half a million dollars should aim to save about $16,000 a year. Someone who is 55 and hopes to save another $300,000 should aim to save about $25,000 a year.

This table can help you work out your own annual savings target. You can write this figure on the seventh and last line of the retirement planning worksheet.

You now have your plan.

The approach is similar if you are planning to send a child to college.

Table 2.1   Retirement Calculator

Age	Savings Goal by Age 65			
	$100,000	$250,000	$500,000	$1,000,000
20	$ 700	$ 2,100	$ 3,600	$ 7,200
25	900	2,300	4,700	9,300
30	1,200	3,100	6,100	12,300
35	1,600	4,100	8,200	16,400
40	2,200	5,600	11,200	22,400
45	3,200	8,000	16,000	31,900
50	4,800	12,000	24,100	48,100
55	8,100	20,300	40,700	81,400
60	18,300	45,700	91,400	183,800

Table 2.2   College Calculator: What You Need to Save Each Year to Reach $60,000 by Age 18

Age	Amount
0	$ 2,300
1	2,500
2	2,800
3	2,900
4	3,000
5	3,300
6	3,700
7	4,100
8	4,700
9	5,300
10	6,100
11	7,200
12	8,500
13	10,500
14	13,400
15	18,300
16	28,100
17	57,400

*Assumes 4 percent real return a year, and college costs rising by 2 percent real.

Table 2.2 looks at how much you would need to save each year, based on the child's age, to reach $60,000 by age 18. It assumes you're starting from zero.

This is based on the estimated cost of sending a student to the state's public university. Sending him or her to a private college will, on average, cost just over twice as much.

These numbers may look higher than some other estimates. But that's because we are using more conservative assumptions. That gives you a better chance of reaching your goals, and lower risk you will fall short. I'd rather plan for 4 percent returns and be pleasantly surprised to get 6 percent than the reverse.

You may get substantially more than 4 percent a year in real terms. But you may not. Indeed you may get less. There are no guarantees.

In that case even these savings targets will leave you short of your target. But these numbers are based on reasonable, and pretty conservative, assumptions.

Part of the challenge of saving for college is that there really isn't that much time—less than 20 years after the child is born. It's a good reason to start as soon as possible. Those saving for retirement, if they start early enough, may have more time.

How Can You Move the Numbers in Your Favor?

Working through this simple process is going to force a lot of people to face some hard truths. Too many have saved far too little and are unprepared for the future.

The most powerful thing you can do to build your financial future is to raise your cash generation as high as you can. That's the subject of Chapter 6.

But for some, these targets may simply be unachievable. That's especially true for those who are older, nearing retirement, and still way short of their goals.

If you can't hit the target, here is some modest good news: You can try moving it. There are a couple of techniques that investors should be aware of that can help you nudge the numbers in your direction.

Scale Back Your Plans

Take another look at the goal.

Changing your expectations in retirement can have an outsized impact on your financial needs.

Once you are retired and you are effectively your own boss, you will have a lot more freedom about where to live. You may also have more control over other costs.

Fred Brock, the author of *How to Retire on Less Than You Think* (Times Books, 2004), argues it's possible to enjoy a great retirement without spending the earth. Among his tips: moving to parts of the country where living costs are low.

He has a point. The expensive real estate is near the high-paying jobs. The cost of living varies a lot across the United States. There is a terrific calculator, using survey data known as the ACCRA Cost of Living Index, at Bankrate.com (you can find it at www.bankrate.com/calculators/savings/moving-cost-of-living-calculator.aspx).

Living costs in many places (e.g., Austin, Texas; Portland, Oregon; and Cincinnati, Ohio) are a fraction of those in the most expensive cities. (This is also particularly true regarding assisted living facilities and nursing homes. The costs are far lower in the less expensive areas of the country.)

You don't even have to go that far afield to save money. You can just move further beyond the commuter belt.

People with jobs really don't want to travel more than about an hour each way to commute each day. So they tend to crowd in and around the major cities, where the highest-paying jobs are, and they bid up the prices of real estate in those areas.

Once you get more than about an hour's travel from the city, prices suddenly drop off a cliff. You get a lot more for your money. That can be a huge saving with little difference to your actual quality of life.

After all, if you cut your real estate costs by $500 a month, that will save you $6,000 a year. That's the equivalent to adding about $120,000 to your retirement account.

You can also change the numbers sharply if you keep earning, as well. Even a part-time job paying $10,000 a year can change the retirement math dramatically.

Even quite small changes to your retirement costs will have a disproportionate effect on your savings goal. Why? It's because your Social Security (and other pension) payments won't change.

Imagine a couple, both 50 years old, who think they will need $50,000 a year in retirement but expect Social Security payments of $20,000. Obviously that means they will still need to generate income of about $30,000 a year from their own resources. To do that, they should aim to save about $600,000 before they retire. If they want to retire in their midsixties, they will probably need to save about $30,000 a year.

Now imagine they decide they can live in retirement on $40,000 a year instead of $50,000.

That's a 20 percent cut in income. But their Social Security payments will stay the same. So the extra income they will need to generate will fall by a third. And so will the annual amount they need to save each year; it will drop from $30,000 to $20,000. That's a lot more achievable.

One further point: Money we save each year has to come out of our disposable income. We need to pay living costs and taxes first. We can save only from what's left over. So cutting your savings target by even a few thousand dollars a year can have an enormous effect on your quality of life.

Delay Your Goals

You can also help your situation by moving your goals back a few years to give yourself more time to save.

This isn't so easy with some objectives, such as sending a child to college. But when it comes to retirement it's one of the most powerful things you can do.

It's a four-way win. For every year you delay the day you retire and start taking Social Security benefits, you:

1. Give yourself an extra year to save.
2. Give your savings an extra year to grow.
3. Cut the amount of time you will need to live off your savings.
4. Get a bigger Social Security check when you do retire.

The fourth benefit is the real kicker. The Social Security Administration is grappling with the financial costs of the nation's rising life expectancy. That's why it penalizes early retirees and rewards those who delay. Just delaying Social Security from 62 to 66 may increase monthly payments by about a third, and delaying it to 70 may raise them by 80 percent or more (Figure 2.3 shows sample benefits for someone who will turn 62 in 2017).

If delaying the date you start taking Social Security boosts your annual benefits by $5,000, then it cuts around 20 times as much, or $100,000, from your savings target. If delaying boosts your benefits by $10,000, then that should cut your savings target by $200,000.

According to the Social Security Administration, most workers take Social Security before they turn 66. Nearly half take it at age 62, the first year they are eligible. In many cases it's a foolish move. As more and more people come to grapple with the financial challenge of retirement, this can be expected to change.

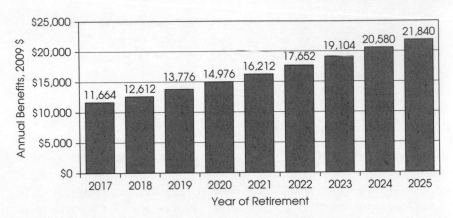

Figure 2.3 How Delaying Retirement Can Increase Social Security Benefits
Source: Social Security Administration web site (www.ssa.gov).

Consider the math for a 50-year-old woman, earning about $50,000 a year, who's hoping to retire at 62. Let's say she figures she will need about 75 percent of her current income, or $37,500 a year, in order to retire comfortably.

She finds that if she starts taking Social Security at 62, her payments will come to just $13,300 a year. That will leave her with about $24,200 a year that she will need to generate from her own savings.

Twenty times that is $484,000. To save that in 12 years (in order to retire at 62) is hardly possible. If she earns 4 percent above inflation, she'd have to save $32,200 a year. She earns only $50,000.

But if she delays retirement and taking Social Security until she is 66, the numbers change sharply. She will get an extra $5,000 a year from Social Security. Thanks to the rule of 20, that knocks $100,000 off her savings target. And she has four more years of saving to get there.

Now, instead of trying to save $32,200 a year, she only has to save $17,600. That's a big drop. But out of an income of $50,000 a year it's still probably impossible.

If she waits another four years, until she is 70, the gains are even bigger. Her Social Security payments will rise to $25,000 a year. The amount she will have to save each year to make up her income shortfall drops to just $8,400.

That's barely a quarter of what she needed to save to retire at 62. It's hardly easy, but it may just about be manageable.

And I haven't even factored one extra benefit: Someone who retires at 70 needs their savings to last for eight years less than someone who retires at 62.

Rethink Your Estate

Another way of moving the numbers is to take a look at insurance products that will convert your savings into a lifetime income, although this may leave nothing for your heirs. A single-premium immediate annuity (SPIA) may squeeze extra income out of each dollar you have saved, because it transfers longevity risk to the insurance company. In its purest form you simply buy an annual income for life, and that's what you get—whether you live for only two years or for 40. It's like buying a pension.

The downsides? Life insurance products can embed significant fees, which eat into your returns. With most annuities you hand over control of your money. If you find you need a lot of cash quickly after all, you may be out of luck. And the typical SPIA leaves nothing for your heirs: It's an income for life.

The fixed payments of most SPIAs also leave you at the mercy of inflation: Your income will lose purchasing power over time. You may also be at the mercy of the insurance company's solvency. That's a risk. Each state has a so-called guaranty fund to backstop policies if an insurance company fails, but the amount protected per policy is capped. If you take out a policy, make sure you stay within limits.

SPIAs differ. Some leave a benefit. Some guarantee a certain number of payments if you die early. Some will provide an income until both spouses die. Some offer inflation protection. But each of these benefits comes at the expense of a lower income, sacrificing the main advantage of an annuity.

One newer alternative worth a look is so-called longevity insurance. These policies kick in with an annual income only if you live past a certain age, often 85. That means you can run down your savings from 65 to 85, knowing that if you live longer your insurance policy will cover you. This, too, is another way of trying to squeeze more annual income out of your retirement savings.

These alternatives aren't for everybody. But if you are struggling to square the circle of retirement needs and your current savings, they may help.

Incidentally, if you were hoping that the idea of an inheritance would keep your children and grandchildren eagerly attentive during your golden years, you can still do this cheaply. Just make occasional knowing comments in their presence about "the money" with a slight smile. Young people are quick to accept that the elderly have vast wealth squirreled away, even if there is no obvious sign of it. They will figure you may have a fortune in Apple stock, purchased in the early days and locked in a safe-deposit box somewhere. The idea should keep them on their toes and the birthday visits flowing. And by the time they find out there is no pot of gold after all, you'll be dead anyway.

Conclusion

- Too many people have saved too little and borrowed too much. They are hoping for Santa Claus to turn up—and he isn't coming to town.
- To be prepared for your financial future you should start with a plan. It's much like planning any journey. Choose your destination, check where you are now, and then work backwards from the destination to find the route.
- If you are saving for retirement, you could start by estimating you will need about 75 percent of your current income to maintain the same standard of living when you retire.
- Deduct the income you can expect from Social Security and any other pension sources. What's left is the income you will need to provide from your own resources.
- You'll probably need about 20 times that annual income to make sure it will last a full retirement.
- The markets come with few guarantees. Contrary to what you may have been told, longer-term investments may not earn much more than 4 percent a year over inflation.
- If the annual savings target seems too high, think about scaling back your goals, delaying your plans, or rethinking your legacy.

Retirement Planning Worksheet

Retirement income you'll need	$ _____
Less: Likely Social Security and pension income	$ _____
Subtotal: Retirement income gap	$ _____
× 20 = Retirement savings target	$ _____
Less: Current net worth	$ _____
Savings gap	$ _____
Annual savings goal	$ _____

CHAPTER

The Basics

Most people are financially exposed to the elements. They have little or no protection. The next steps in protecting your finances involve fixing that.

This chapter takes a look at three important steps to securing your financial position. You need to:

1. Break out of debt.
2. Secure your lifelines.
3. Cover your risks.

Break Out of Debt

If you are carrying a balance on a credit card, you are not free. You are living in servitude to your lenders. It's that simple.

Credit card debt is one of the biggest rip-offs on the planet.

The typical card balance is about $3,000, according to the Federal Reserve's 2007 Survey of Consumer Finances. But that shades the real story: A substantial number of people are carrying a lot more than that. Those card balances have risen even while more people have bought their own homes and taken on mortgages as well. Overall, the average debt burden of the American family has doubled in 20 years.

Breaking out of these chains should be your number one priority. It's far and away the smartest financial move you can make.

(There is one exception to this rule, and it became a source of controversy during the financial crisis of 2008. If you are so deeply in debt that you think personal bankruptcy is a serious option, paying off your card or cards might be exactly the wrong thing to do. You might be better off contributing as much money as possible to retirement plans, such as your 401(k), where it will be safe from creditors. It's a complex topic. I'll look at this in greater detail in Chapter 7. But unless you are in such dire straits, normal rules apply and your top financial priority should be to pay off your cards as quickly as possible.)

As long as you are carrying credit card debt, you can't start saving and accumulating the wealth you need to retire in comfort, or to help the children go to college. How could you? You're paying 12 percent or more on the money you owe. And that's in after-tax dollars. You have to make 14 percent or more gross (depending on your tax rates, of course) just to stay level. Wall Street figures it had a good year if the stock market went up 10 percent.

It makes no sense whatsoever to invest in shares while carrying a balance on your credit cards. Worrying about your investments, or speculating on stocks in the hope of making a big score, is a total waste of time.

As long as you are carrying a balance on your credit cards, you are working for everybody but yourself. Your employer. The card company. And the government. You have to pay all your taxes before you pay interest.

You may end up getting only 50 cents for every dollar's worth of work you do.

It's no surprise many card companies dropped the minimum monthly payment levels back in the 1990s. They don't want you to pay that card off. They want to keep you on the hook.

At 12 percent interest, if you have a typical $3,000 card balance and just pay off the minimum 2 percent a month, it will take you 22 years and two months to clear the debt. Over that time you will pay $3,179 in interest. To put it another way, the $3,000 in purchases that landed you with the debt will end up costing you more than $6,000. (To do the math for your own cards, check out an online calculator like the one at Bankrate.com.)

If self-interest doesn't get you focused like a laser beam on paying off your cards, maybe getting mad will. Think about where your money is going:

- U.S. banks made $13 billion in 2004 just from the late fees on credit cards.
- Card interest isn't even tax deductible. You have to earn $1.25 or more before tax to pay $1 worth of interest.
- According to a report published by the Federal Reserve Bank of Boston, credit card companies celebrated tough new bankruptcy laws in 2005 by lending more money to marginal customers, as they knew customers would find it harder to escape.
- The chairman of Visa, Inc., makes $10 million a year.
- Hoping to beat Wall Street? Here's your chance. Paying off your card is like making 14 percent or more before tax. Wall Street is lucky to achieve 10 percent in a year.
- The CEO of credit card giant Bank of America, makes about $20 million a year.
- Between 2006 and 2008, American Express chief executive Ken Chenault took $1.1 million worth of personal flights on the company's private jets. What was your last vacation?

There are good ways and risky ways to pay off your cards. The good ways are through cash generation and, maybe, by cutting your withholding tax. The risky ways are through borrowing money against your 401(k) or your home.

Generating cash means spending less than you earn. In Chapter 6 we'll look at ways to get there as fast as possible. This should be the first place to look for the money to pay down your debt. When it comes down to it, the only reliable source of cash flow in your life is you. Your ability to generate positive cash flow is your greatest financial resource.

Most of the discussion about generating cash will wait until Chapter 6. If you are in credit card debt, everything in that chapter counts double.

There are two things you can do to help yourself. But they come with risks.

The first: See if you can transfer that card balance to a new card that will give you an interest holiday.

Card companies frequently offer this to woo new customers. And they should be really eager to sign you up. If you are carrying a balance on your current card, they will consider you a perfect mark. They'll want your business.

The problem: Many people will use the new card to borrow even more. That, of course, is going to make matters worse, not better. Anyone who thinks they might follow suit would do best to avoid new cards.

But if you are making serious efforts to pay off your debts, a transfer like this can help. It can stop the interest clock for six months or even longer. The extra savings can help you pay off what you owe.

Uncle Sam might also be willing to help you pay off that debt.

The average credit card balance is about $3,000, according to the Federal Reserve, as mentioned before. Bankrate.com says the average interest rate is about 12 percent, though many people are paying a lot more. So the average interest bill runs to maybe $300, or a little more, a year. (And then there are the late fees. . . .)

But about three-quarters of income tax filers get a refund each year. The average, according to the Internal Revenue Service (IRS), is about $2,500. Or nearly as much as the average credit card balance.

Do the math: A lot of people are effectively borrowing from the credit card company at 12 percent, and simultaneously lending most of that money to the federal government at 0 percent. This isn't a paying proposition.

People cheer when they get a tax refund, but it just means they paid too much withholding tax. You don't actually owe those taxes until the end of the year.

If you are in this situation each year, you can make a quick saving by cutting the payroll taxes withheld from your paycheck at work. Just contact the payroll department and file a new W-4. That's the form that helps them estimate the amount of income tax you're likely to owe at the end of the year. If you raise the number of dependents on the form, the amount that's deducted will go down.

There are some automatic limits. For example, under IRS rules, anyone who declares 10 or more dependents on their W-4 is likely to face an automatic query. (That's a lot of dependents.)

You can use that money to start paying off your credit card immediately. Those who cut their withholding too low, and don't make up the difference until they file their taxes on April 15 the following year, will face a penalty. It's 5 percent. The irony: That's probably a lot less than the interest they're paying on their cards. (Caution: This is a risky game. The same amount of taxes will still have to be paid in due course. The imprudent will think this is free money and spend it.)

In addition, individuals have a responsibility to try to produce an accurate estimate of how much tax they are likely to owe.

There are two even riskier ways to pay off your cards. You may be able to borrow money from your 401(k) plan at work at a low rate of interest. And you may be able to borrow against your home, through a bigger mortgage or a home equity line of credit. Again, the interest rate will be much lower than the one you are paying on your cards.

Both of these options may seem seductive and appealing. After all, why not borrow against your 401(k) at, say, 6 percent and pay off the debt that's costing you 12 percent? Not only is the interest rate on the 401(k) plan lower, but you'd be paying it to yourself anyway. What's not to like?

Think twice before making either of these moves.

First, there is a point of principle. Treating your home and retirement savings as sacrosanct in this matter is a good discipline. It will force you to pay off your debts out of what you earn. Too many people got into the easy habit of living off their retirement savings or the equity in their homes. Because they took the easy route, they never changed their way of life. In many cases they kept tapping their home equity to pay off their credit cards, and spending more, until there was no home equity left.

But that's not the only reason to be wary of this move.

Your 401(k) plan is a key part of your financial fortress. As we will see in Chapter 7, it is a sheltered, protected asset. As long as you leave money in there, creditors cannot touch it. In many cases your home, too, may enjoy the same privilege. It may be protected against unsecured debt, such as the money you owe on your credit cards. But it will not be secured against a mortgage or home equity line of credit.

Loans from a 401(k) come with a particular peril: If you lose your job, you may have to pay it back straightaway—or the IRS may deem it a taxable withdrawal and hit you with taxes and penalties.

Consider two people who each owe $30,000 on their credit cards (an extreme case, but illustrative). Each also has $50,000 in her retirement plan. The first person borrows from her 401(k) to pay off the cards. The second doesn't. Both lose their jobs and are out of work for a long time, a fate that has befallen a lot of Americans lately. What happens?

The woman who borrowed from her 401(k) is left with just $20,000 in her retirement account. The second person? She files for bankruptcy. The credit card debt is wiped clear. She faces no extra taxes or penalties. And she gets to keep the $50,000 in her retirement account.

One final thought on credit cards: If you have been carrying a balance on your cards, you can do yourself a huge favor by cutting them up and going without them altogether. Cards make it way too easy to spend. They encourage impulse shopping and they let you spend money you don't have. It's an addiction; it's as simple as that.

Secure Your Financial Lifelines

What would happen to you if you lost your job tomorrow? What would you live on? What would you do if you couldn't get a job for another year or even longer? Or if you had to work part-time, for minimum wage?

The following two figures tell the story. Figure 3.1 shows the underemployment rate—the number who were either unemployed or forced to work part-time because there wasn't enough full-time work to go around.

Obviously the numbers are alarming. But perhaps even more worrying is the volatility. When it comes to jobs, the tsunami hits suddenly, and without much warning. Within a matter of months in

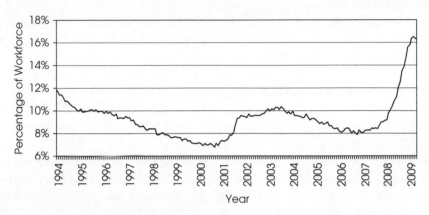

Figure 3.1   U.S. Underemployment Rate from 1994 to 2009
Source: U.S. Department of Labor,

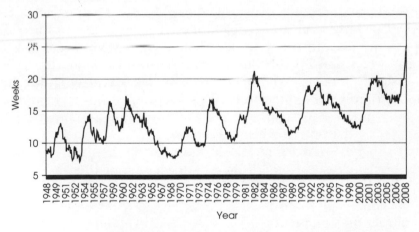

Figure 3.2   Average Time Out of Work, U.S. Unemployed, 1948 to 2009
Source: U.S. Department of Labor.

2008, for example, the number of long-term unemployed trebled. Such volatility has not been seen since the Great Depression.

Meanwhile, the unemployed are also spending a longer time out of work, on average, than before. As Figure 3.2 shows, the trend has been rising for a generation.

What does this mean for your finances?

You need to know where your emergency financial lifelines are. You need to know where you can get access to the cash that you need to live at short notice.

Some commentators recommend you keep three to six months' worth of living expenses in an emergency fund. During the financial crisis some advisers raised the ante still further, and urged families to keep up to nine months' living expenses in a bank account.

But there's a problem with that.

According to the U.S. Department of Labor, the average American household spends about $42,000 a year. Three months' expenses would be about $10,500. Six months' would be $21,000, and nine months' would be more than $30,000.

But if a typical family sets this kind of money aside in a bank account as an emergency fund, that would probably constitute most—or all—of their savings.

And bank accounts, especially those you can access quickly, are very poor long-term homes for money. The interest rates are low (that's the price you pay for a federally guaranteed account with quick access and no volatility). Furthermore, the interest is taxed as ordinary income. When you factor in taxes and inflation, this money simply isn't going to earn its keep. Far from it. Instead of beating inflation by maybe 4 percent a year or even more, it is going to be hard-pressed just to keep up.

To suggest that families keep most, or all, of their savings in this form in case of emergencies is to condemn them to a poor retirement.

There are alternatives.

Focus on emergency *lifelines*, rather just emergency *funds*. It is almost certainly a needless waste to keep all of your emergency money in a bank account. But you may not need to, either. You simply have to know how you can reliably get access to sources of money, even in a financial crisis, should you need to.

No solution is perfect. It is a question of balancing risks.

In addition to holding money in the bank, here are five other options to consider. Each one has its own risks.

1. Conservative stocks and bonds.
2. Home equity line of credit.

3. Margin debt.
4. Your individual retirement account (IRA).
5. Card debt.

Conservative Stocks and Bonds

Even when you want to keep some money where you can reach it easily, you don't have to keep it all in a low-yielding bank or money market account. You can keep some of it in longer-term investments. Unlike cash accounts, stocks and bonds do fluctuate in value. But so long as they only make up part of your emergency reserves, that needn't be too much of a problem. And they may give you much higher returns with only a bit more risk.

In the case of stocks, stable, blue-chip companies with high dividend yields can be a good home for some emergency funds. Their returns over time are likely to be better than a bank account. And stock dividends are lightly taxed.

It's best to stick to companies that are less sensitive to economic cycles, like utilities and those in consumer staples. Their shares are less likely to suffer badly in a slump.

Banks, and other highly cyclical stocks, are best avoided in this area.

In the case of bonds, the most suitable are municipals, high-grade corporate bonds, and Treasury bonds issued by the federal government.

It makes sense to stick to short- or medium-term bonds, too. Very long-term bonds, including those issued by the government, can be more volatile in price.

The problem with Treasury and corporate bonds is that their interest payments count as taxable income, just like those in a bank account. And if you hold them in a tax shelter, such as an individual retirement account, you may get penalized for early withdrawals. (There are a few escape clauses, and of course you can make withdrawals freely after 59½.)

Municipal bonds, on the other hand, may fit the bill.

These are bonds issued by states, cities, and towns. The most secure are known as general obligation bonds, or GOs. They are backed by the "full faith and credit" of the city or state that issues them. This means they'll raise taxes, if they have to, to pay the coupons. (Almost as good are high-rated bonds backed by essential services, such as town water systems.) Such bonds have almost never defaulted. The interest payments on municipals are exempt from federal income taxes and those in the issuing state. That makes them a good home for emergency funds.

These small differences can make a big difference over time. In the 15 years through December 2008, taxpayers who kept their money in tax-free medium-term municipal bonds would typically have ended up with about 25 percent more than someone who kept it all in taxable one-month certificates of deposit (CDs).

Munis are not as perfectly stable as a bank account. Their price varies. There was a period during the 2008 crash when they took a hit, too. But it's worth keeping this in perspective. Even in the depths of the worst financial panic since the Depression, the iShares S&P National Municipal Bond exchange-traded fund, a bellwether for munis, fell only about 10 percent. And it recovered in a few weeks.

Munis, of course, make sense only if they are offering a higher yield than the one you would earn, net of tax, in a bank or other high-grade bonds.

Home Equity Line of Credit

If you have excellent credit and a lot of equity in your home, a home equity line of credit (HELOC) can be a useful financial lifeline in a pinch. The interest rate should be very low, because the loan is secured against the value of your home. If you have good relations with your bank and you set up the credit line when you don't need it, you should be able to tap it quickly.

But it's not without risks. During the credit crunch banks reeled many of these lines in—just when the customers needed them. And as a HELOC is secured against your home, the danger is obvious. What if your financial situation does not recover quickly? What if it gets worse? You can lose your home if you end up defaulting on a loan secured against it.

Margin Debt

You may also be able to borrow money from your broker, using your investments as collateral. It's called margin debt.

This is another potential source of short-term funds, but it shouldn't really be an early line of defense. Margin debt is typically more expensive than a home equity line of credit. And it comes with another complication.

Many of your investments are likely to fall sharply in price during a financial crisis. That means you won't be able to borrow as much. And your broker may demand repayment quickly. Brokers, unlike mortgage bankers, will watch the market value of your assets constantly. If your shares or other investments fall too far, the broker may demand more money, or may force you to sell some of them to shore up the account. There are also limits to the amount you can borrow against investments. Margin debt is really only appropriate as a backstop. But it's there.

Your Individual Retirement Account

Ordinarily I am not a fan of taking money out of your retirement accounts. That money is sheltered from creditors, as well as from taxes, as long as it is in there. And in most cases early withdrawals run the risk of substantial penalties.

But you should at least know your options. One that may be important in certain emergencies is called a substantially equal periodic payment (SEPP). You can withdraw a certain amount per year from your IRA without paying penalties. There are complex technical ways of calculating how much you can withdraw. The payments will be based on your life expectancy and annuity tables. They need to be about the same each year and continue for at least five years. You will need to talk to your IRA provider to organize it and make sure it complies with the rules. But it's another source of funds.

Of course if you are over 59½ you can withdraw money without penalty from your 401(k) or IRA. You can also make penalty-free withdrawals before that in certain circumstances.

Credit Card Debt

This is going to be controversial, and it needs to be clear that this should be a last resort when other options have been exhausted. If you are in a deep short-term crisis, you may be able to borrow money on your cards, or spend money on them and carry a balance. Obviously this is not recommended in most circumstances. As I mentioned earlier, the interest rates are generally usurious. Credit card debt is bad for your wealth. But those who dismiss credit cards as a last resort are misunderstanding the law. Credit card debt is unsecured lending. Even if you file for bankruptcy, the card lenders will probably be unable to touch your retirement accounts. As we will see in Chapter 7, if you take the right steps to protect your home they may not be able to touch that, either. This might be called a last resort lifeline.

Check Your Big Risks

After every flood, homeowners tend to rush out and buy flood insurance. Obviously this is the worst possible time to buy it. The smart move is to buy flood insurance when the land is dry and the skies are blue. But who thinks of it?

A detailed look at the issue of insurance is beyond the scope of this book. But securing your financial position also means making sure you are covered against the major risks that could threaten it. Many people are overinsured against minor risks, like a fender bender, yet happily walk around with little protection against major risks like disability.

That means conducting a risk audit to understand your key vulnerabilities, and considering how to protect them. Flood damage may be the least of your worries.

Insurance is the broccoli of financial planning. Maybe it's good for you, but who cares? So here are two reasons to give it some thought. It's easy to underestimate risks before they happen. And it's also easy to assume you are already fully covered, only to find out, too late, that you aren't.

And it's not about trying to eliminate all risks. Insurance can be expensive. In many cases you may be better off saving the money than spending it insuring a minor risk that you can deal with yourself. The main task is to insure against the major, catastrophic risks.

In the case of homeowners' and car insurance, many people simultaneously have too much and too little coverage. On the one hand, they set their deductibles too low in order to insure themselves against small costs. This is a very poor use of money. Raising your deductibles can slash your annual premiums.

At the same time they may set the upper limits on their claims too low. So while they are protected, very expensively, against small costs, they are simultaneously left exposed to very big ones. This is the wrong way around to do things.

A quick risk audit involves three simple steps.

1. Identify your major risks.
2. Check your current coverage.
3. Fill in the gaps.

Life Insurance

If someone depends on you financially—a spouse, a child, an infirm relative—then you should consider taking out life insurance. You may have some already through work. But check the terms and the coverage. It may not be enough, or the best deal.

Work out how much insurance you need: how much income, or a cash payout, your dependents would need if you died. If you have children, that may include the money you would want them to have for college. If you have a nonworking spouse, it may include helping with your spouse's retirement needs.

Life insurance comes in many varieties, but the simplest, and usually the best value, is straightforward term life. This simply covers you for a period of time, which can be up to about 30 years.

Other forms of life insurance, such as whole life and variable life, add an investment component on top of the insurance. That way you may get money back at the end. Insurance products are rarely the best investment products, although they do get some tax advantages. Remember, when it comes to insurance, there are no freebies. Insurance companies can't pay out more than they take in. So if they are giving you more back, they have to charge you more. If you are simply trying to cover the risk that you will die early, term life is the most efficient way to do it.

Disability Insurance

You are more likely to suffer an injury that keeps out of work for a long period than you are to die prematurely. That raises fresh financial risks. If you are disabled you may stop earning, but you will still need money to live.

You may be relying on Social Security disability payments to cover you. But these are more limited and restrictive than many realize. You may also have disability insurance through work. Again, you should check the coverage. It may be far less than you think. You may want to consider buying extra insurance yourself. It's usually sold through a broker who specializes, and it can be expensive.

There are several key questions to ask about any policy.

Will it cover you if can no longer do your own job ("own occupation" coverage)? Or will it cover you only if you can't do any job ("any occupation")? What is the waiting ("elimination") period before you can claim benefits? How much income will it replace, is it taxable, and how long do the payments last?

Homeowners' Insurance

Make sure your coverage is complete and up to date. It may have gaps you haven't considered.

Have you installed a new kitchen since you bought the policy, or built a sunroom on the back? If so, you may need to raise your coverage to include that. Have building costs risen locally? And that's also true if construction costs have risen a long way. If you took out the policy many years ago, the assumptions you used may be out of date.

Does your policy cover the full replacement cost of your possessions, or just the lesser cash value? The latter means the insurance company deducts a certain amount for depreciation.

Are your most valuable belongings fully covered? There may be limits to the amount you can claim per item, or per category. If you have a lot of valuable jewelry, say, or silverware, you may need to add a special rider to make sure they are covered.

Do you have a recent inventory of your possessions? It's a lot harder to put one together after a burglary or a fire than it is now. The easy approach: Take a video inside your home, moving from room to room and showing everything you need covered.

What is your liability coverage? You can buy an umbrella excess liability policy to raise it. That can make sense in many cases, especially if you have significant wealth or you are, for example, professionally vulnerable to lawsuits. If you have a home office, you may also need extra coverage or a business-in-home rider.

Homeowners' insurance rarely includes flood damage. If you are in an area where that is a real danger, it is worth considering separate flood insurance.

If you are a renter, many of the same rules still apply. You should check to make sure you have the appropriate renters' insurance to cover your most important possessions and liability risks.

Car Insurance

The biggest risk to check in your automobile insurance policy is your third party liability, especially if you are in a state with a low mandatory minimum. You may want to raise the limits.

A second risk is that you will get into an accident with a driver who lacks money or full liability protection. That can leave you with difficulty dealing with medical bills and other costs. You can buy a special policy to insure against uninsured and underinsured driver risk.

The third risk is that of damage to your car. This is the one risk that many people overinsure. We will look at that in Chapter 6.

Long-Term Care Insurance

If you are in your fifties you may want to give thought to long-term care insurance. Many people assume Medicare will cover them. But the coverage is actually very limited.

It is a complex form of insurance. As with disability insurance, it's worth seeking out a broker who is experienced in this line and who deals with multiple carriers. As ever, understand his or her commission structure, too. You may be able to get coverage through your employer.

Issues you'll need to think about include the maximum amount you can claim per day, and the length of coverage. There are no easy answers. The average stay in a nursing home is less than three years, but of course in some cases it can last many more years.

Conclusion

Protecting your financial future stars with some basic steps. In this chapter we looked at three.

1. *Breaking out of debt.* If you are carrying a balance on your credit card, you simply aren't free. Most of the value of the work you do goes to other people. Breaking free of that debt as fast as you can by paying off those cards should be your number one priority. Until you do that, few other financial moves will help you.

2. *Securing your lifelines.* Disaster can strike quickly. You should make sure you have secure access to financial reserves in case it happens to you. Ideally you should be able to tap at least three to six months' living expenses. But keeping the money in a bank account may not be the most efficient use of it. The interest rates are likely to be low and they are taxable. Consider holding some of your reserves in conservative, high-quality stocks and bonds instead. And focus on ensuring you have cash lifelines, rather than necessarily keeping it all on hand as ready money.

3. *Checking your insurance.* Everyone faces risks that could hit their finances, from a fire or a car accident to a long-term disability. It's a good idea to conduct a risk audit, to make sure you have the coverage you need for your major risks. Insurance, and insurance policies, is complex. Remember that insurance products are usually financially inefficient. The smart approach is to buy the coverage you need, use high-deductible plans, and don't confuse insurance with investment.

CHAPTER 4

How Not to Invest

Successful investing is like driving. Most of it is actually about avoiding accidents and staying on the road. As many have discovered, that's a lot harder than it sounds.

What exactly went wrong? Why have so many investors ended up in the ditch? And what can they do to avoid that fate in the future?

Much of the answer lies in the immediate past. The quarter century from 1982 to 2007 saw the biggest bull market in recorded history. The Dow Jones Industrial Average rose nearly 15-fold. House prices nearly trebled. Investments and assets around the world soared.

It was natural that, sooner or later, many investors would come to think this was normal, and to plan accordingly. After all, the people who prospered during this period were those who took big risks. They kept all their money in stocks, and they bought more when shares went down. They bought real estate and borrowed as much as they could. Meanwhile those who acted more cautiously missed out.

But this period wasn't normal. This was the exception. Markets, as everyone has rediscovered, can go in both directions.

It's no surprise millions of Americans have lost faith in their investment strategies as a result. Many are confused. Some are hiding in cash. Others have fled to government bonds and even gold coins. But it's a case of old myths being replaced by new myths. Any investment strategy based on simplistic assumptions is heading for trouble.

This chapter looks at many of the things that went wrong, and the mistakes many investors are still making.

Putting Too Much Faith in Stocks

You frequently hear that "stocks always outperform over the long run," usually coupled with the proviso that "they are more volatile."

But it's too easy. Yes, stocks can often be an excellent investment. But their miraculous powers have been overstated.

Stocks are not the only place to have your money. And their potential depends enormously on the price you pay for them.

When you make an investment, you are just securing a claim on future dividends or interest payments. That's true whether you are buying a bond or a share or a certificate of deposit (CD) at your bank. How much you should pay depends on how many dividends or interest payments you can expect, over what time period, and how certain they are.

Stocks, Bonds, and Everything Else

A stock or a bond is just a claim on a future income stream. Shares generate dividends. Bonds generate coupons. This is the only source of their value.

Stocks outperformed other assets in the past because they were undervalued. It's as simple as that. They were cheap compared to their future dividends. But once the Dow Jones Industrial Average had risen from 1,000 to 10,000, as it did from 1982 to 1999, that was no longer true.

During the boom, more and more books encouraged people to put their trust in the stock market. One well-known example: Jeremy Siegel's *Stocks for the Long Run* (Irwin, 1994; 2nd ed. McGraw-Hill, 1998). Professor Siegel teaches at the Wharton School, one of the world's top business schools. His book, which included data going back to 1802, argued that shares had beaten inflation pretty consistently over two centuries by an average of about 7 percent a year. For anyone investing over a period of 20 years or so, he concluded, the stock market was almost always the best place to have your money.

Yet those who knew their stock market history could recall an ominous echo. Professor Siegel's main argument, and even the book title, resembled that of an earlier best seller—*Common Stocks as Long-Term Investments*, by Edgar Lawrence Smith. The year that was published: 1925. Smith's earlier book encouraged many to invest during the mania that led to the 1929 crash. Professor Siegel would later be blamed, by some, for something similar.

There are problems with this simplistic argument in favor of stocks.

First, the long-term performance of shares may not be as good as supposed. The data is subject to some technical disputes. As my *Wall Street Journal* colleague Jason Zweig has pointed out, the earlier data, especially from the nineteenth century, simply isn't reliable. And where the argument depends on the performance of U.S. shares during the twentieth century, it is subject to an additional bias: This was the golden age of American capitalism. U.S. companies cleaned up while overseas competitors were devastated by two wars and imperial decline. There is no reason to assume these circumstances will continue.

Other economists, including Elroy Dimson, Paul Marsh, and Mike Staunton at the London Business School, have looked at a century's worth of data for both U.S. and foreign markets and found that the typical returns of shares were lower. An annual return of 5 percent over inflation, instead of nearly 7 percent, may be nearer the long-term average.

That's a huge difference. If you invest $100 at 7 percent over 30 years, you will make about $660 in profits. Invest it at 5 percent and you'll make only about $330—just half as much.

And that's especially important because shares, of course, are volatile. So if the average return is lower than expected, there's a much greater risk that you will actually lose money over 10 or even 20 years.

There is a further problem. You can expect similar returns to the historic average only if you buy shares at roughly average valuations.

How often people seem to forget this simple, and obvious, point. If everyone buys stocks, and they rise too far, they will become overvalued. From that level they will no longer do as well. This is what happened in the late 1990s, and again in 2006 to 2007.

It's also worth adding that long-term performance data really applies only to really long-term investing, too. The stock market may take decades to outperform.

The baby boomers poured money into Wall Street in the late 1990s. They were hoping to build up their nest eggs quickly before retiring. But they should really have been ramping up their investments earlier.

Shares aren't simply volatile. They also tend to be volatile at exactly the wrong times—namely, when the economy plunges into turmoil, people lose their jobs, and they need their savings. This is exactly what happened during the crash of 2007 to 2008.

Stocks for the long run became stocks for a long face.

Whenever shares are booming, the airwaves are filled with experts arguing that they will go even higher. It is natural for the public to assume the experts' forecasts are reliable. But this is not always the case.

Ordinary investors need to understand that stock market analysts are almost always optimistic about shares, even when that is the wrong opinion to hold. And they are most optimistic at exactly the times they should be pessimistic. The period 1999 to 2000 was the peak of the biggest bubble in Wall Street history. It was one of the best moments of all time to sell all your shares. Yet a study by the *Financial Times* found that most analysts' recommendations at the time were to buy stocks, not to sell them.

Every major bankruptcy has been preceded by a last-minute rush as the analysts desperately drop their positive recommendations. (Whenever a major company's stock has crashed from $50 to $2 and its imminent bankruptcy is in the headlines, look for news about some Wall Street analyst announcing, "We have downgraded our rating from long-term outperform to hold.")

Technology stocks in 1999. Bank stocks in 2006. At the peak of every bubble, just when you should be selling, the experts are usually bullish. Back in 2005, when the housing bubble was at its peak, home-building stocks soared to unprecedented valuations. It would prove to be the greatest moment in history to sell them all. Despite this, as I noted in my *Boston Herald* column at the time, the Wall Street analysts covering these stocks were at that moment generally very bullish.

The public may not realize it, but a stock analyst's recommendation has to be treated very differently from, say, a movie review.

If every critic raves about a new movie, it's probably worth seeing. But if every analyst praises a particular stock, it may actually be worth avoiding. That's because the word is already out. Investors have probably already bid up the price of the shares.

> ### Going Against the Grain
>
> Ordinary members of the public often feel reassured to find themselves in the company of experts. But when it comes to investing, they should be worried. If at the crucial moment experts agree on something, it probably means that investors have already stopped asking tough questions.
>
> - In 2006 and 2007 many bankers and analysts were positive on banking stocks, subprime and developers.
> - In 2005, at the peak of the housing bubble, almost all the analysts who covered homebuilding stocks were bullish about them.
> - In 2000, when the stock market was at its peak, the vast majority of analysts were bullish about stocks, and hardly any research notes advised selling your shares—even though that turned out, in many cases, to be the right thing to do.

And so it is for markets, too. The biggest risk is to invest when things are going really well. Everyone's optimistic. And shares are likely to be expensive.

In June 2007 the top institutional investors around the world told a survey by Merrill Lynch that they were incredibly bullish about European stock markets. Prices seemed good and the economic outlook seemed wonderful, they said. Merrill dubbed the mood "EU-phoria." I wrote at the time that if previous instances were any guide, this would be a terrific moment to sell all your European stocks.

And so it proved. European markets promptly plummeted. Far from being the best place in the world to hold your money, they proved to be some of the worst. Some markets fell by two-thirds in the carnage that ensued. EU-phoria felt more like EU-thanasia.

This sort of paradox is quite normal in the markets. The worst investments are typically the ones everyone loves. And the best are the ones everyone hates, including the experts. (All the gold analysts were gloomy in 2000, when gold was $260 an ounce. Everyone was most bearish about the Japanese stock market at the lows, in 2003.)

There is another problem with putting too much money in the stock market. Most people won't get the full benefits anyway. That's because many of them just can't hang on through the turbulence.

From 1986 through 2006, the stock market, including dividends, produced average returns of about 11.8 percent a year. But the average stock market investor made only about 4.3 percent, according to an analysis by Dalbar, Inc., a financial analysis firm.

Why was the return for the average investor so low?

Investors bailed out after the market slumped. And got back in once it was booming again. Over and over.

Yes, people panic. No, perhaps they shouldn't. But to blame this all on the clients is merely a new version of an old refrain: The clients are always wrong.

Are those who sell during a crash being irrational? Maybe not. Maybe they just can't afford to lose half their savings. Especially when, after the market has fallen 50 percent, there is no guarantee it won't fall another 50 percent. (During the panic in the fall of 2008, billionaire Warren Buffett urged people to buy stocks. As *Saturday Night Live* joked, there was no reason to panic . . . so long as you were already the richest person in the world).

Someone with $40 billion can lose half of it and still get by. Somebody with $40,000 can't.

Japan's slump began in early 1990 and after nearly two decades still hadn't ended. After 1929 Wall Street didn't regain its former level until 1946, 17 years after the crash. And another bear market on Wall Street lasted all the way from 1969 to 1982, while the market lost two-thirds of its value in real, inflation-adjusted terms. If that happens to your retirement savings shortly before you retire, you may spend your golden years packing bags in the supermarket. If it happens to junior's college fund, junior may end up going to refrigerator college. So what if those investments are likely to outperform in the next generation? How will that help you?

A pure equities strategy simply isn't appropriate for most people.

Forget the academic studies. To try to compete with the stock market indexes in the real world is folly. The stock market has infinite time and infinite money. It never has to send children to college and it never has to retire. It never loses its job. It can ride out decades of misery if need be. Few individuals are so lucky.

Putting Too Much Faith in Phony Diversification

Too many people think they are magically safe because their money is diversified across U.S. and emerging markets stocks, large-cap value stocks, mid-cap growth stocks, and small-cap blend stocks. After all, that's what countless experts have told them.

The problem? It doesn't always work—as many investors found out in 2008.

In that year, shares in emerging markets fell 50 percent. U.S. shares fell about 40 percent. Large-cap value: down about 36 percent. Small-cap blend: down 36 percent. Mid-cap growth: down 45 percent. Everything except U.S. government bonds collapsed.

China was supposed to be safe because it was allegedly decoupled from the slowing U.S. economy. But Chinese shares fell 49 percent. Brazil was supposed to be safe. The economy was booming. But the São Paulo exchange fell 41 percent.

What went wrong?

This isn't real diversification. Mid-cap growth isn't even an asset class. It's a marketing label. Ditto large-cap value, small-cap blend, and the like. As long as mutual funds have to keep all their money in shares and can only bet that shares will rise, they are not diversified. They are just variations on the same investment.

Faith in this type of diversification dates back at least to Harry Markowitz, a Nobel Prize–winning economist in the early 1950s.

He was the founding father of what is called modern portfolio theory, the reigning dogma in the finance industry. Professor Markowitz argued that investors should own lots of different assets that were uncorrelated—in other words, that had nothing to do with each other. This, he said, could give you better returns with less volatility. So someone who invested in small U.S. company stocks and, separately, in emerging markets stocks was likely to be better off than those who had all their money just in small U.S. company stocks.

Up to a point it has worked. Markets and industries have boomed and slumped at different times. Investors have often found that Tokyo or Hong Kong was rising while Wall Street was in the dumps. Oil companies raked in record profits while the computer industry hemorrhaged cash. When telecom, media, and technology stocks crashed in 2000, old-line value stocks, like beer companies and local banks, boomed.

But this theory suffers from four big flaws.

First, it relies way too much on recent history. Global markets in the modern sense have been operating for only a handful of decades. This is hardly enough time to provide a guide to the future—as anyone who understands history could tell you. (It's no coincidence that Wall Street, and the finance industry, is packed with math and economics majors. They're big on extrapolating, but they don't know much about history.)

Second, it works only as long as your uncorrelated assets stay uncorrelated.

But in the age of globalization, these asset classes have become like teenagers on prom night. It's getting tough to keep them apart.

In 2006 and 2007 many portfolio managers tried to avoid the coming credit crunch in the United States by shifting their clients into emerging markets funds that invested in overseas countries like China. The theory, which became an article of faith among portfolio managers everywhere, was known as decoupling. The idea was that the economies of the emerging markets would decouple from the overborrowed United States.

But if the overborrowed U.S. consumer stops shopping, guess what happens to a shoe factory in Shanghai that makes shoes for Wal-Mart?

Decoupling, my eye.

When the subprime crisis hit, China actually fell further than Wall Street. One reason: So many investors worldwide needed to liquidate their holdings. These days, increasingly, there is one global financial market. To talk of individual stock markets—London, New York, Hong Kong, Mumbai, Tokyo—is becoming a little beside the point. A lot of the money in these markets is managed by the same big global institutions, and they can move it around at the click of a mouse.

Third, the one thing that actually goes up in a crash is the degree of correlation. Different assets may rise differently, but when the crunch comes they all fall together. So diversification helps you least just when you need it most.

Fourth, and finally, this theory works only if some assets are cheap while others are expensive. Shares in old-fashioned companies like cigarette companies, brewers, and small banks boomed after the dot-coms collapsed in 2000. But they didn't boom by magic. They boomed because their shares were very cheap. The reason they were very cheap was that everyone had been ignoring them in the mad scramble for dot-com shares. So it wasn't part of an unrelated phenomenon. It was part of the same phenomenon.

If you have a worldwide bubble and all shares go through the roof at the same time, the diversified investor just ends up holding a broad basket of overpriced assets. That's what happened in 2007. And it offered no protection.

Taking Too Much Risk

Alongside the blind faith in the magical power of stocks, and blind faith in the magical power of diversification, is the blind faith in the magical power of risk.

Many people believe they can easily earn higher returns by taking on more risk and volatility. They are often encouraged in this belief by certain sections of the finance industry. The wreckage left by this theory can be seen in investment accounts up and down the country.

There are two problems with the idea.

First, nobody actually knows how much volatility they can handle until they have been through it. True, many portfolio managers and financial advisers hand out "risk tolerance" forms when you first arrive to elicit an answer: "I am willing to tolerate a loss for higher long-term returns—yes/no/maybe," and so on.

But asking someone with no experience of stock markets about their attitude to "beta" and "volatility" is box ticking at its most absurd. It's as silly as those immigration forms that ask people if they plan to overthrow the government. In many cases the purpose is to protect the adviser from later lawsuits, not to protect the client from the stock market. As one of the greatest writers on finance, Fred Schwed, once wrote, nothing can really prepare you for what it feels like to lose money you used to own.*

The clients and advisers may not even agree on what risk actually is. Those in the finance industry, especially if their own money is not at stake, think it is something called volatility. The clients know it is actually the danger of losing money.

The second problem is even more profound.

Taking on more risk in this simple box-ticking way may not even earn you higher returns anyway.

It is common to hear people in finance say things like "Small-cap stocks generate higher long-term returns than large-cap stocks, but they are riskier," and "Investors with a higher risk tolerance should have more money in international stocks." Such comments are so frequent that if you tune in to any financial program on TV you might hear a string of them within a matter of moments.

But they're hooey. Do you believe in magic?

How can anyone possibly judge the risks or potential returns of an investment without knowing the price you paid? It's absurd.

Blame modern portfolio theory, which argues that the highest long-term returns come from the most volatile assets.

But a share is simply a claim on future dividends. How much you pay for it makes all the difference.

Some will tell you that small company stocks, on average, have produced higher returns over many decades than large company stocks. But all that means is that small company stocks were under-valued during that time. After they had doubled in price, which is what they did between 2003 and 2007, that was probably no longer the case.

---

*Fred Schwed Jr., *Where Are the Customers' Yachts?* (1940; repr., New York: John Wiley & Sons, 1995).

Dynamic, fast-growing stocks are often described as "riskier" and "more aggressive" investments that will produce higher returns with more volatility. Yet over many decades they have usually produced lower returns than baskets of duller, steady-Eddie value stocks that cannot boast much growth but enjoy high company profits and pay big dividends.

The reason? Most of the time, these growth stocks have been overvalued. Investors, excited by companies with big hopes for the future, have shown a pronounced tendency to pay too much for them. Meanwhile they have underappreciated value stocks. No one wanted them, precisely because they were too dull.

In other words, the risks and returns of growth and value stocks haven't simply been the product of the fundamental nature of the companies themselves. They have also had a lot to do with how cheap or expensive these stocks were in relation to future dividends.

This led to a curious turn of events from 2005 to 2007, which surprised more people than it should have. Many investors reversed their usual bias. There was a vogue for value stocks on Wall Street, while growth stocks fell out of favor. (Baby boomers, nearing retirement, were told by some advisers that value stocks entailed lower risks.)

What happened next?

When everyone rushed to put all their money into value stocks, they became overpriced. And when the market began to crash, the inevitable occurred. These overpriced value stocks ended up falling much further than growth stocks.

Small company stocks are often called risky, but they can be extremely safe and conservative investments if you buy them cheaply. That can even be the case for companies that sound highly speculative. In 2002, amid the wreckage that followed the dot-com collapse, many former Internet highfliers were left as little more than shell companies. Yet in some cases their shares traded for less than half the value of the cash that the companies had sitting in a bank account. Is that a risky investment?

If large-cap value stocks are so safe, then how come those who bought General Motors, Merrill Lynch, Lehman Brothers, Bear Stearns, Cisco Systems, or Polaroid at the wrong prices lost most or all of their money?

There is no magic. Warren Buffett, the world's second-richest man, is famously cautious about investing. You could call him very risk-averse in many ways. It doesn't seem to have lowered his returns. He has about $40 billion, all of it made through investing.

Misunderstanding Your Mutual Funds

Mutual funds are a great idea in theory. Investors get together, pool their money, and hire a smart manager to navigate the waters of the financial markets on their behalf.

But that isn't how it works in most cases. Most funds aren't smart funds, where an intelligent manager has broad freedom and flexibility to maneuver. Most are dumb McMoney funds. The manager is trying to run your money the way McDonald's makes hamburgers.

Why? Because the marketing department tells him to. McMoney funds may be mediocre, but they are easy to sell to the public.

No wonder McMoney funds do so badly. If the people in the marketing department knew beans about investing, they wouldn't be in the marketing department.

During the crash of 2008, so-called actively managed stock market funds, where a manager was supposed to be looking after your money, actually fared slightly worse than the funds that simply followed the market index.

Let's look at some of the typical mutual fund's flaws.

They Can't Hold Cash

The most powerful weapon in any fund manager's arsenal is the ability to sell shares and keep some of the money in cash if he or she cannot find good enough investments at a good enough price. Insisting that a manager invest all the money, all the time, is like demanding that a baseball player swing at every pitch or a poker player bet on every hand. It is a near guarantee of mediocrity.

Yet that's what most fund companies do. Your typical mainstream stock market fund, known as a diversified equities fund, has to be fully invested in the stock market at all times.

Their public explanation? "We don't try to time the market." It's a good enough piece of spin to fool a lot of the public a lot of the time. And if it fails during a market crash, no problem: Most other fund companies are doing the same thing, so investors have nowhere else to turn.

"You can't time the market" is a line you hear over and over from the money industry. It is extremely self-serving.

It works as a warning to the clients, to keep them fully invested in mutual funds, and as an excuse, to explain why their funds were fully invested when the market collapsed.

Yes, research shows that over time most of the stock market's returns have come from just a small number of days. So it's a big gamble to get out of shares completely. But there are plenty of options between 0 percent and 100 percent.

Valuing a Share: The Price-Earnings (P/E) Ratio

One of the most common ways of valuing a share is to compare the price to the year's earnings, or after-tax profits, per share. This is the so-called price-earnings (P/E) ratio. Historically, the average for the stock market overall has been about 14 times earnings. At the peak of the late 1990s boom, though, valuations rose far higher. It was one sign that shares were overvalued and a poor investment.

Wall Street Price-Earnings Ratio, 1985 to 2009

Data source: Copyright 2009 FactSet Research Systems Inc. All rights reserved.

And the research isn't all one-way. For example, a study at the IESE Business School in Spain looked at 16 years' worth of returns for 15 international stock markets and found that if you had simply missed the 10 biggest one-day jumps out of 160,000 days, you would have cut your overall profits by 50 percent.* But missing the

Valuing the Market: Price-to-Sales Ratio

Another way of valuing the stock market is to compare share prices to the annual revenues of the companies. The so-called price-to-sales ratio is a simple measure—but it can be surprisingly useful. It can help make massive overvaluations, such as occurred in the late 1990s, pretty clear—as the chart shows. Revenues are less volatile than after-tax earnings. So they are less likely to get deceptively overinflated in an economic boom, or vanish, misleadingly, in a recession. That makes them a somewhat steadier yardstick to measure the stock market against.

Wall Street Price-to-Sales Ratio, 1985 to 2009

Data source: Copyright 2009 FactSet Research Systems Inc. All rights reserved.

---

*Javier Estrada, IESE, "Black Swans, Market Timing, and the Dow,"*Applied Financial Economics Letters*, 2008.

10 *worst* days would have *raised* your profits by about 50 percent. So being out of the market needn't be fatal at all.

And while you may not be able to time the market from a trading point of view, that does not prescribe the fatalism that some portfolio managers would suggest. You can still reach some intelligent conclusions about the price of the market. You can avoid stocks and markets that are obviously overvalued.

Historically, those who have invested in the stock market when it has been cheap in relation to company profits and dividends have earned much better returns than those who have invested when it was expensive. Yale economics professor Robert Shiller has shown that the returns you're likely to get over any 10-year period on Wall Street are pretty closely related to how cheap the market was when you invested.* To most people, that may sound like common sense.

They Are Handcuffed to Benchmarks

Mutual funds have mandates. Most are required to invest in a certain style. It's laid down in the prospectus. It's in all the marketing materials. It's the basis on which all those portfolio managers invested their clients' money. And woe betide the fund manager who deviates.

No matter what is happening in the markets, or the dangers they may see ahead, they may not be able to take evasive action.

It's like being told that the captain of the *Titanic* saw the iceberg ahead but wasn't allowed to turn because the White Star Line had put out a brochure saying it would follow a certain route.

As I mentioned earlier, most mutual fund managers have to stay fully invested in the market at all times, regardless of what they expect. They aren't allowed to keep much or any money in cash. Many of them aren't even allowed to look around for the best opportunities, either: They can only invest in a certain type of stock or a certain style. If a fund manager is running a small-cap value mutual fund, that's all he can invest in: small-cap stocks with a so-called value profile. It doesn't matter whether he thinks all such stocks are terrible bets. It doesn't matter if he gets a call one

---

*Robert J. Shiller, *Irrational Exuberance* (Princeton, NJ: Princeton University Press, 2000).

morning from a large-cap growth company offering his clients free money. He is duty-bound to ignore it. He has to stick to small-cap value, no matter what. That's his mandate.

This absurdity reached its nadir during the late days of the dot-com bubble in 1999 and 2000. Contrary to what you may hear, lots of fund managers knew perfectly well at the time that the market had gone crazy and that the prices of technology stocks were ridiculous. Many of those running growth and technology funds could hardly think otherwise. They were, after all, the ones taking meetings with 22-year-olds who had drawn up their business plans on the back of an Applebee's menu and were asking for a billion dollars.

But even though these fund managers knew the market was absurd, there wasn't much they could do about it. They were required to keep their funds fully invested in these so-called growth stocks at all times.

Iceberg dead ahead, captain.

Full speed ahead!

The fund managers could shrug their shoulders and assume that the clients were managing the risks. But in many cases the clients weren't. The clients didn't know the latest technology initial public offering (IPO) from a bowl of nuts. The clients weren't taking the meetings with 22-year-olds or seeing these business plans. They were leaving that up to the fund managers.

During the summer of 2007, when emerging markets were rocketing to new highs, I spoke to a fund manager who specialized in investing in Asian markets such as China. He described to me scenes from a recent trip to Shanghai that clearly showed it was turning into a gigantic bubble. Indeed, at the time I compared it to the last days of the dot-coms.

But still he had to keep his funds fully invested in these markets.

These so-called style boxes, like mid-cap blend, large-cap growth, and international, started out as a useful way of sorting out the many thousands of mutual funds on offer. But the identity bracelets have become handcuffs. The manager of a mid-cap growth fund has to stick pretty much to shares in middling-sized companies with a growth portfolio. If that manager sees lots of great investments among very large companies or very small ones, too bad. And heaven help international fund managers whose experience and intelligence lead them to find excellent values among U.S. stocks (or vice versa). They'll get their knuckles rapped for the alleged crime of style drift. Perhaps you've never heard of such a thing, but it's considered a cardinal sin in money management. The accusation may come from clients, clients' advisers, portfolio managers, the marketing department, or from firms like Morningstar and Lipper that track and analyze mutual funds.

During the 2008 crash, many mutual fund managers actually took a perverse pride in the fact that their funds lost so much money. It showed they had done exactly what they were supposed to do. They had stuck to their benchmarks. They had followed their style right over the waterfall, just as they had promised.

Chasing Performance

Tracking mutual fund sales is depressing. The public rushes to buy funds that have just had a good run, racing to "get on board" and "back the guy with the hot hand." It's foolish. Studies have found that the fund managers who have just beaten the market for six months are more likely to do worse over the next six.

As for the three- or five-year averages: If there's any way to use this information, it's to bet against it. If the best-performing funds over the past five years are, say, those that invest in industrial manufacturing companies, and the worst are those that invest in pharmaceuticals, lots of people will dump their pharmaceuticals funds and buy industrial funds. It's a terrible idea. Statistically, you are actually more likely to make money doing the exact opposite.

A surprising number of investors look at stocks and bonds upside down. They think a share that has fallen a long way is becoming a worse deal, and one that has risen is looking better.

Sometimes I will write about a share that looks like a good value because the price has fallen a long way. Invariably I'll get e-mails from people who tell me I am an idiot because this share is a terrible investment. "If you'd bought it last year, look at all the money you would have lost," they write.

Technology funds had the biggest sales right at the peak of the bubble in 1999–2000. Those mutual fund managers who had the freedom to maneuver, and who correctly avoided technology stocks,

Don't Give the Market Too Much Credit

As an investor it's easy to get spooked by volatility. If a share jumps or falls sharply, it's tempting to assume there's a good reason for it. Beware of putting too much weight on the short-term movements in the market. There are lots of things driving them. Oftentimes they don't mean very much for a long-term investor.

Consider the case of Kellogg, Inc., the breakfast cereal company. In early 2004, the stock market valued the entire company at just over $16 billion. By the middle of 2008 that had risen all the way to $22 billion, an increase of nearly 40 percent. By early 2009, after the crash, it had fallen by nearly half to below $14 billion—even less than it had been worth five years earlier. Yet what happened to the business over that time? It just grew, slowly and steadily. Sales rose from $9.6 billion to $12.8 billion, and pretax profits from about $1.4 billion to $1.6 billion. The wild movements on the stock market didn't tell you much about the underlying business.

often got badly punished for their wisdom. The clients walked. A few managers got fired—for being right.

This wasn't unusual. In 2005 Andrea Frazzini from the University of Chicago and Owen Lamont from Yale Business School studied 23 years' worth of data on how ordinary investors had switched money between mutual funds. Their conclusion? From 1980 through 2003, the public typically switched funds at the wrong time. They sold the ones that had done badly just before they started to do well. And they bought the ones that had recently done well just before they started to do badly. The researchers called retail investors "dumb money" and calculated that someone could have made good money just by doing the opposite of the investing public.*

No wonder so much of the fund management business now spends its time behaving stupidly. It is pandering to fickle consumers who don't actually understand what they are really buying.

---

*Andrea Frazzini and Owen Lamont, "Dumb Money: Mutual Fund Flows and the Cross-Section of Stock Returns" (working paper, National Bureau of Economic Research, September 2005).

Trying to Find the Next Apple

Too many people spend far too much time picking individual stocks. It's true that many shares may go up even when the stock market doesn't. But good luck trying to find them.

Few professional fund managers outperform the market. It's not entirely their fault (see the preceding discussion). But it shouldn't exactly fill you with confidence, either.

Even if you do succeed, chances are it won't be by much.

During the boom years, lots of investors tried to beat Wall Street.

Peter Lynch, the former manager of Fidelity's Magellan Fund, launched a whole generation of stock pickers with his popular books *One Up on Wall Street* (Simon & Schuster, 1989) and *Beating the Street* (Simon & Schuster, 1993). My old colleague Jim Cramer— "Booyah!"—made stock ownership fun with his popular cable show *Mad Money*.

When times were good, the risks were lower. If your portfolio went up 12 percent in a year you were probably pretty happy—even if Wall Street overall went up 14 percent.

How much difference a bear market makes.

A lot of people looking for a home run struck out.

It's easy to see the appeal of trying to manage your own stock portfolio. It puts you in control of your own money. It allows you to take advantage of obvious opportunities, and to dodge obvious icebergs. It liberates you from the marketing departments at McMoney mutual fund companies. It lets you manage risk.

But it is incredibly hard to do in practice.

Investors live in their own Lake Wobegon. Each one thinks he or she is above average, or that their portfolio manager is. It's rarely true.

There are very few successful fund managers, even among the professionals. Studies show that about 80 percent of them actually do worse than a simple index fund over time. Intelligence isn't enough to pick stocks. It usually takes years of formal training and decades of experience. It takes certain personality traits, too. Intellectual brilliance or mathematical genius probably help. But iron self-discipline and patience are usually even more important.

Successful investing is a temperamental challenge more than an intellectual one. The great investors will sit on their hands for years.

And it is a full-time job, even when the job consists of nothing but reading research materials and deciding not to invest in anything.

What are the problems with building your own portfolio? Individual stocks involve a lot of risk. Anything can go wrong with a single company. People can also get emotional about stocks. No one gets emotional about a mutual fund, and that makes it more likely you'll make cool, calm decisions about your investments. That isn't half the battle. It's about nine-tenths.

One of the biggest problems is that too many private investors try to find the next Apple. It's a terrible strategy. While a few of these ventures will succeed, most will flop. People always boast about the one that made them a lot of money. They rarely mention all the others.

Overall, you're better off owning shares in the most boring and stable companies you can find. As I mentioned earlier, glamorous growth stocks are usually overpriced. Boring ones are more likely to be undervalued. Hardly anyone wants them.

James Montier, formerly the global strategist at SG Securities in London, looked at this phenomenon in the U.S. and European markets from 1985 through 2007. He considered first the so-called stars of the market: the companies that had grown profits the most in recent years, and were forecast by analysts to keep doing so. Then he looked at the so-called dogs—those that had grown profits the least, and were forecast to do no better.

Bottom line? The dogs trounced the stars. Indeed, the stars actually ended up doing much worse than a plain old index fund—while the dogs did better.

(Someone who invested in the dogs in the United States gained 14.9 percent a year, compared to just 13.4 percent for the overall market. The stars? They made only 9.9 percent. In Europe the dogs returned an astonishing 19.5 percent a year, while the market made 14.3 percent and the stars 12.4 percent.)

Private investors often put far too much emphasis on capital gains, and too little on dividends. Capital gains—the stock that goes from $10 to $50—look and sound exciting. But over long periods of time, reinvested dividends have traditionally provided the lion's share of the stock market's returns. Investing in stocks with high and sustainable dividends is a far better strategy than investing in stocks you hope will rise.

Boring old value stocks make more sense for individual investors than glamorous, go-go growth stocks for another reason: You don't have to keep so much of an eye on them. The news doesn't tend to change too much from day to day. Big detergent companies and regulated utilities don't tend to go from hero to zero overnight the way software companies do (though of course anything can happen).

If you buy a high-flying stock, it is simply uncanny the way it will come out with disastrous news just as you are away on a two-week safari.

Investing in stocks brings other concerns. If people are devoting time and energy to trying to pick individual shares, they are probably not paying enough attention to the questions that really matter, and where they can make a real difference—like whether they have too much money in equities, and how to save more.

Even if you don't lose your shirt on individual stocks, any underperformance is costing you. It's deadweight in your portfolio.

And of course investing in shares involves far more than deciding whether you like a company or its products. It depends on the share price and the company's financial position. Even in the case of a pretty straightforward company this can be surprisingly complex.

Most individual portfolios end up badly imbalanced, a haphazard jumble of legacy stocks and ill-chosen additions. You'll probably have too little money in the shares that do well and too much in the ones that do badly. There are far better things you can be doing with your time than trying to catch the next Apple or Google.

Owning Shares in Your Employer

Many people think they are at least safe owning shares in their own employer. After all, you work there. So that should be okay, shouldn't it? In some cases you may get a discount when you buy the shares, too.

Alas, this is the riskiest investment you can make. Especially if you are dependent on your employer for your career.

Many Americans took this gamble and have now been completely wiped out as a result. When the company got into trouble they were two-time losers. They lost their savings—and their jobs.

Ask the staff at Washington Mutual (WaMu) if this was a good idea. Or those at Lehman Brothers or American International Group (AIG) or Citigroup. Or Fannie Mae, Bear Stearns, or Polaroid.

You are already heavily invested in your employer, even before you buy a single share of company stock. That's because you work there. There is no reason to ratchet up your risk still further by putting your savings in the same place.

Do the math.

Someone hoping to earn $50,000 a year from their employer for the next 20 years already has the equivalent of a $600,000 investment in the company. Why? That's roughly how much they would have to pay for an annuity that would produce a similar income stream.

The two are not exactly alike, of course. An annuity doesn't require you to show up at the office every day. But they are alike in the one thing that really matters: You are counting on the income.

That's some investment. Do you really need some stock on top?

Yet many people continue to risk a lot of their savings by investing in their own employer's stock. Indeed, where the company 401(k) allows it as an investment option, more than half of the participants put some money into company shares, and a small minority effectively bet the farm.*

Why do they do it?

For many, it's probably a case of false logic.

Some will talk about colleagues who "made a lot of money" from company stock. So what? The question is whether they could have made the same, or even more, by investing elsewhere. Others will tell you they're holding the stock because the company is doing very well. Yet the stock market almost certainly knows that already. Public companies have to report results every three months, and frequently update the market even more often. So most good news is already factored into the share price, which will be correspondingly

---

*Employee Benefit Research Institute, *Issue Briefs*, January 2009.

high. Others say they are hanging on to their stock because "it's undervalued" and "it has to rise." But everybody says the same thing about their company. They can't all be right. Overinvesting in your own employer is simply another version of the oldest mistake: keeping all your eggs in one basket.

Still others will take confidence from the actions of the top executives, who may have a lot of wealth tied up in stock and options. They must know what they are doing, right?

It's crazy. Senior executives are usually rich and professionally secure. If everything goes to hell they will land safely somewhere else. And they tend to have much bigger cash reserves to fall back on outside the company. Sure, executives may have $100 million in paper wealth tied up in company stock. But they may have $20 million elsewhere, plus the house in the Hamptons and the yacht. And the kids may have long since completed college. In that case they are taking a much smaller risk than the frontline worker with even $50,000 in company stock.

Keeping All Your Money in the Bank

It's a big mistake to keep all your money in the bank because it's safe. Bank accounts and certificates of deposit (CDs) usually come with federal insurance. But they are not really as safe as they may look. It's an illusion. On the contrary, as I mentioned earlier when we looked at emergency funds, over long periods of time bank accounts have been poor homes for your money.

Blame inflation and taxes.

Too many savers and investors get suckered by a money illusion. If they're getting 3 percent interest on their money they think they're doing well, even if everyday prices are rising by 2 percent—or more.

Inflation is a sneak thief of money. It's much more important over time than many people realize. In 1967 a pound of roast coffee cost about 76 cents. By 2007 the price was $3.60.

A loaf of bread went from 22 cents to $1.40.

Over that period the average cost of everyday goods rose sixfold. So even if your money rose by the same amount it was just keeping up.

What does this mean for you? Take a look.

Over the past 40 or so years, money kept in short-term CDs has earned an average compound interest of about 5.6 percent a year. Sounds good?

Alas, over that same period consumer prices have risen by an average of about 4.6 percent a year. The real interest on this money was around 1 percent.

And of course anyone keeping their money in the bank had to pay tax on the interest, too.

Taxes are especially bad when they interact with inflation. Why? If you earned 5.6 percent interest in a bank account, but consumer prices rise by 4.6 percent, then of course you have hardly gained any ground at all. Your money won't buy you much more coffee or many more donuts this year than it did last. But try telling that to Uncle Sam. As far as he's concerned, you're up a full 5.6 percent. And he wants a cut. You have to pay taxes on it.

The government doesn't tax you on the real, after-inflation return on your money. It taxes you on the nominal or illusory return. If you are paying 15 percent tax on 5.6 percent interest, you're getting to keep only 4.8 percent. In real terms you're making no return at all.

When you count both taxes and inflation, someone keeping their money in the bank may not be making any gains at all. They may actually be paying for the privilege of saving their money for a rainy day.

Figure 4.1 tells the story. It shows how these numbers would affect someone who kept $100 in a CD or savings account over 40 years.

The top line is what she thinks she is getting. Her initial $100 investment grows to about $880. That looks like a terrific return.

The bottom line is what she may actually be getting. If she is paying a typical 15 percent tax rate on her interest, and consumer prices rise by around 4.6 percent a year, her $880 would actually only be worth $109 in today's money.

She saved $100 for 40 years and got back $109 in real, inflation-adjusted dollars.

Some may object, by the way, that this inflation rate is too high. The inflation figures from the past 40 years include very high numbers in the 1970s and early 1980s. But of course CD rates were

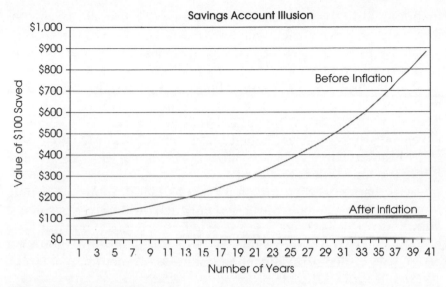

Figure 4.1   The Cash Illusion
Sources: Federal Reserve, Bureau of Labor Statistics.

also high during that period to reflect that. If inflation turns out to be lower in the future, so will the interest rates in the bank.

Keeping All Your Money in Bonds

In the wake of the stock market crash, a lot of people were urged to put more of their money in bonds. It's common to hear things like "Bonds are safer than shares, but they offer lower returns." And it's often true. But it's not the whole answer. It also depends on the price you are paying. Many bonds have actually produced much higher returns than shares for years, because the bonds were cheap and the shares were expensive.

Bonds are simply IOUs. They can be issued by almost any institution that needs to borrow money, from the U.S. Treasury to individual corporations to your local school.

They have a lot to commend them. Bonds and bond funds can often give you extra income and stability. They frequently offer higher interest payments than the dividends on shares. But they still come with risks. Some bonds are at risk from default. And many, including most government bonds, are at risk from inflation. No bond is a completely safe home for your money if you pay too much for it. It's astonishing how many people, including professionals, sometimes forget that.

For example, U.S. Treasury bonds are generally referred to as "the safest investment in the world" and a risk-free investment. These are bonds issued by the federal government. True, the U.S. government has never defaulted on its debt. Obviously Uncle Sam owns his own Mint, so he can always print dollars to pay his bills. But that is only part of the story.

What happens when inflation rears its head? Someone owning long-term Treasury bonds will certainly get the interest payments, known as coupons. But those will buy less and less. Someone who bought a 20-year Treasury bond in 1965, just before inflation took off, actually ended up losing money on the investment in real terms.

So much for "safe."

The federal government in 2008 launched an unprecedented wave of deficit spending to keep the economy from meltdown. It has flooded the economy with new money. Such actions have typically led to inflation.

During the depths of the financial crisis in 2008 everybody and their Aunt Sally rushed out to buy Treasury bonds in a frenzy. Inevitably they drove up the price of those bonds to ridiculous levels. As most bonds pay a fixed rate of interest, when the price goes up the effective interest rate falls. (It's often compared to a seesaw—when bond prices rise, the yield falls.) In this case the yield on the 30-year bond fell as low as 2.6 percent a year. That's little more than half the interest rate you might expect. Anyone buying such a supposedly safe bond was actually taking a very risky gamble that inflation would stay low for decades to come.

Within a few months such bonds had slumped. Investors lost money.

Short- and medium-term bonds are less at risk from inflation than long-term bonds and therefore less volatile. That means bonds that are due to mature within 10 years. The shorter-term the bond, the less the risk. As a result they also offer lower returns as well.

Bonds aren't just "safe" or "risky." How safe or risky they are depends on both the type of bond and the price you pay for it.

> ### Bonds and Risk
>
> All long-term bonds are at risk from inflation. All nongovernment bonds are at some potential risk from default.

Stockpiling Gold

If you have ever had insomnia, you may have seen the commercials. Gold merchants peddling the crazier conspiracy theories tend to advertise on late night TV, right between the *M*A*S*H* reruns and real estate infomercials starring Erik Estrada. You can also hear them on the AM dial of your radio in the small hours. The arguments are doubtless popular with those stockpiling guns in the Idaho panhandle while they prepare for the United Nations to invade. And with those receiving alien transmissions through the fillings in their teeth (gold or otherwise).

Attention turns to gold in every financial crisis. And you will hear the same arguments again and again. It's a "safe haven" and a "store of value." It's a protection against inflation and financial collapse and the only "real money."

It's hard to believe, but at one point during the late fall of 2008 the rush to buy gold was so great that the U.S. Mint actually ran out of its pure gold American Buffalo coins. And of course that news only fueled the panic.

Seems we still have buffalo stampedes in North America. Of a sort.

There is a serious argument for including some exposure to precious metals, including gold, in your portfolio. (More about that later.) But the more extreme arguments are simply pandering to fear and panic. They don't make a lot of sense. And those rushing to hoard bullion are actually taking a deeply risky move.

Consider the arguments you'll hear.

- "Gold is a real asset, while currencies are just paper." Gold is actually no more "real" than anything else. There is no magic to the yellow metal. There is no guarantee that tomorrow the butcher, the baker, and the candlestick maker will accept gold for their wares any more than dollars, yen, a bottle of wine, or anything else. All currencies depend on the same thing: general acceptance.

- "It's been coveted for thousands of years." So what? People in ancient Babylon coveted gold only because there wasn't a lot else around to covet. The iPhone hadn't been invented. The ancients also believed in magic, superstition, slavery, and the divine right of kings. Life has moved on.
- "It protects against inflation." Really? Tell that to someone who bought an ounce of gold at the peak in early 1980. They suffered a bear market that lasted 20 years. Indeed, when you count inflation they still haven't got back to where they were. Gold is actually incredibly volatile. As always, the value of an investment—any investment—depends heavily on the price you pay for it. Ordinary investors may not realize just what kind of danger they are taking on. Figure 4.2 shows what happened to the purchasing power of an ounce of gold from 1979 to 2008. (And this is year-end data. In early 1980 gold soared even higher, to nearly $900.)
- "It's been a constant store of value. For thousands of years one ounce of gold has purchased about 350 loaves of bread." This is simply silly. Should someone who buys Wonder Bread at Stop & Shop for $1.50 pay less for an ounce of gold than someone who gets tomato and basil ciabatta from Whole Foods? And what about those who make their own bread at home? Do they get their gold for free?
- "It's a safe haven in a crisis." Well, yes and no. Gold does generally rise during a panic. But an intriguing research paper published by two academics in Ireland in early 2009 revealed the problem. It reacts too quickly. By the time you've heard about the panic, it's probably already too late to buy gold.*

---

*"Is Gold a Hedge or a Safe Haven? An Analysis of Stocks, Bonds and Gold," by Dirk G. Baur, Dublin City University Business School, and Brian M. Lucey, School of Business and Institute for International Integration Studies, Trinity College, Dublin, February 2009.

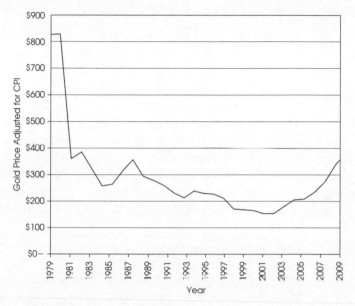

Figure 4.2 Real Gold Price in 1979 Dollars
Source: London Bullion Market Association, 1979–1983, FactSet/NYMEX, 1984+.

There are other dangers with buying gold that don't get enough attention.

- The price is incredibly volatile. In 2008 alone it fell from just over $1,000 an ounce to barely $700. Platinum, another precious metal, more than halved. Anyone who had hoped their gold investments would ensure them a peaceful night's sleep through the crisis must have had a shock.
- Precious metals are actually very difficult to value. If a government bond is yielding 4 percent or a blue-chip stock is paying a 3 percent dividend, you have at least some chance of gauging what you are getting for your money. Is gold cheap at $700 an ounce? If so, why? What about if it rises to $1,000? And if not, why not? The next time it drops 30 percent, should you buy more—or sell while you still can?
- Metals generate no income, either. That means your return has to come entirely from price appreciation. And consider what that means. At the time of writing, in mid-2009, gold

sells for about $900 an ounce. But 30-year government bonds are paying interest of 4.1 percent a year. Anyone buying the gold instead of the bond is betting it will outperform. But just to keep up, gold will have to rise in value to $3,000 an ounce by 2039. To gain 5 percent a year it will have to reach nearly $4,000. Sure, it's possible. So are many things. But it's a bold investor who knows how much an ounce of gold will be worth in U.S. dollars, or any other currency, 30 years from now.

- Finally, and most obviously: If you are buying gold, silver, or platinum directly, you are in danger from thieves. Nothing is easier to steal than gold. Burglars love it. It melts down and is easy to sell. That makes your gold hoard very vulnerable.

Investing Too Much in Real Estate

Many people came to think of real estate ownership as the route to wealth. As soon as they could, young couples tried to save enough for a down payment so they could "get on the real estate ladder." They relied on their home as part of their pension plan.

But, as millions are now discovering, it is far from that simple.

This is not about Monday-morning quarterbacking. No, real estate is not always bad. There is nothing wrong with owning your own home. In many cases it's the sensible move—at the right price.

But too many people assumed it was something more: a guaranteed investment.

A home is a very expensive asset. It probably outweighs the rest of your portfolio by a big margin. Any time you have most of your wealth in a single asset you are very vulnerable. As we have just seen.

It's hard to believe so many gurus advised you to take on extra exposure by purchasing investment properties, too. This is like doubling up at the casino. Of course these are often the experts who said the crash couldn't happen.

(Incidentally, the next time someone holds a $200 seminar at the airport Marriott to tell you how to make a fortune "snowballing" investment properties, ask him why, if it so easy, he spends his time hosting seminars in your local Marriott at $200 a seat.)

Of course, many people insist that real estate is a great investment because you can leverage your money with a mortgage. But that works only as long as your returns from the investment are higher than the interest payment on the mortgage.

The real costs and benefits of home ownership are more balanced. You get any capital appreciation, and the right to live in your home rent-free. But then you have to deduct plenty of costs. There's your interest expense. Taxes. The transaction costs of buying and, later, selling the home. And all the running costs, including insurance, maintenance, condo fees, and the like. And, importantly, the cost that most people forget about: the money you could have made investing your down payment in something else.

The interest rate on the mortgage may be critical. The same home could be a great deal with a 5 percent mortgage and a poor one if you have to pay 7 percent.

Other problems with real estate as an investment? You can't move it. If your neighborhood gets flooded, hit by storms, or blighted by a local economic slump, you can take your other investments and move. Your house is stuck where it is.

It's also hard to buy and sell. Shares and most bonds can be sold in an instant, whenever the market is open, for as little as $8 a trade. Real estate can sit on the market for months, and transaction costs amount to several percent of the entire holding.

And, of course, real estate is hardest to sell when you actually need to do so quickly—like when the economy tanks and you lose your job.

Most investments, like stocks and bonds, pay you something for owning them. At times, it is true, they do not pay you much. But they do generally pay something. The worst that can happen to either of them is that they stop paying you. They never actually charge you annual upkeep. Stockholders in Enron and Washington Mutual lost their money when the companies went bankrupt, but at least they aren't still getting a monthly bill for repairs.

Real estate costs you money every year. So many investment properties have been cash flow negative in recent years that sales listings tend to brag in bold headlines whenever a property might be "cash flow positive from day one!"

(You did not need to be a genius or a seer to realize by 2004 that the real estate bubble was going to burst. It was enough to notice that nearly all properties in bubble areas like Florida and Arizona cost far more to own than they could possibly generate in rent. Of course seeing that the market was going to burst was not the same as knowing *when*. It took a couple of years.)

Why would anyone buy an investment that actually burned cash?

"Well, I know it's cash flow negative," people say, "but I figured I'd make money on capital appreciation."

It's ridiculous. An investment rises in value only because outsiders want in. If it's losing money, who is going to want in? Who is going to rush to jump on board a sinking ship? You're left gambling on what is known as the "greater fool" theory of investing: namely that even though you're being foolish and paying too much for an investment, you are hoping you can sell it for more to an even greater fool.

Owning real estate is also a lot harder than, say, owning municipal bonds. The state of California rarely skips out without paying the rent. It rarely drags you into a spat with the state of Nevada about whose dog fouled whose lawn. It rarely wakes you at six o'clock in the morning to tell you the laundry machine has broken and flooded the downstairs apartment.

In the days when prices were soaring, real estate costs didn't matter so much. They were paltry compared to the rising gains. Effectively, real estate used to pay you to own it.

No more.

Too many people thought real estate always goes up in value. Obviously it doesn't.

Sure, Uncle Ernie got a great deal on that condo in Naples back in 1966. But you have to adjust a lot for inflation. And for all the money he could have made if he had invested that money in something else, like stocks and bonds. That's a lot of money.

If you really want to know how well he's done, you also have to deduct all the running costs, year after year.

Inflation has fooled a lot of people. Figure 4.3 tells the story. According to the U.S. Census, the purchase price of a median or typical house was $18,900 in 1964. In 2009 it was $206,000. That sounds like a big gain.

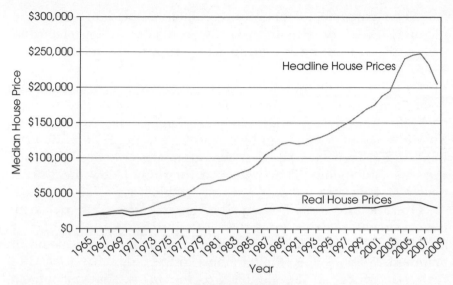

Figure 4.3   House Price Illusion, 1963 to 2009
Source. U.S. Census, Department of Labor.

But most of that was an illusion. Inflation made those dollars worth a lot less. Everything went up, from paychecks to sugar. When you adjust for that, the gain works out at about 1.6 percent a year.

So in 1964 dollars, a typical house in 2009 sold for less than $30,000.

Reality: Real estate prices can fall, in real terms, for years.

Ask anyone who bought a home in Boston at the peak of the real estate bubble there in the late 1980s. According to data compiled by the National Association of Realtors (NAR), it took about a decade for prices to recover to peak levels again. And that was before counting inflation. In real, after-inflation terms, those who bought in 1988 didn't get back to breakeven until 2000, a full 12 years later.

San Diego during the 1990s? About the same.

Or consider the real estate bubble in Houston, Texas, that burst when the price of oil fell in the 1980s. Once again, the story is grim. Someone who bought into the Houston market at the peak, in 1983, had to wait a decade before prices had recovered.

When you look at prices in real, after-inflation terms, the picture is even worse. As of 2007, 24 years later, average Houston prices still had not recovered, in real terms, to the levels seen in 1983.

Or talk to anyone who bought real estate in Tokyo or Osaka in Japan at the peak of the 1989–1990 bubble. Prices didn't bounce back after the initial plunge. They just kept falling. According to a study done a few years ago by researchers at the Federal Reserve Bank of San Francisco, Japanese real estate prices kept sliding into the new millennium. They remain a long way below their peak, nearly 20 years later.

Over the long term, house prices have seemed to rise by a couple of percentage points more than inflation. Karl Case, a professor at Wellesley College and one half of the pair behind the well-known Standard & Poor's/Case-Shiller house price index, has looked at real estate prices all the way back to the 1870s. His analysis: On average, the long-term gains over that beat inflation by only about 2.5 percent a year.

No, it's not always bad. By 2009 you could find some great bargains in the housing crash. But it's not a one-way bet, either.

Conclusion

Too many investors have relied on simplistic assumptions and flawed investment strategies. Many of these strategies survived during the boom only because asset prices were rising across the board. But the period from 1982 to 2007 was the exception rather than the rule. The future is likely to be more complex. Simplistic strategies are unlikely to succeed.

But the bigger issue isn't about any individual asset class. It's that the holy grail of investing is knowing that there is no holy grail. There is no magic secret or formula or key. Not "stocks for the long run" or "bonds for the long run" or "gold coins for the long run." Not "value stocks" or "dogs of the Dow." No system that can be readily replicated can ever outperform. If it could, everyone would follow it, and who would then be left to underperform?

To anyone who has ever tried to lose weight, the truth will be familiar. In investing, as in dieting, there are no magic shortcuts or gimmicks or pills that you can rely on to get you where you want to go and keep you there. There is no alternative to eating better and exercising more.

Or, to put it in football terms, too many people are hoping to win by throwing Hail Mary touchdown passes. Successful investing is like the ground game: slow, hard, and unthrilling; three yards and a cloud of dust.

Drawing lines to extrapolate from the recent past is misleading at best and downright dangerous at worst. You cannot evaluate any investment strategy without knowing the price at which you are investing, and as the future is unknowable no one can know today the price that investments will fetch tomorrow, next month, or next year.

During this chapter I've looked at some of the biggest mistakes that many investors make. To recap, they include:

- Putting too much faith in the stock market—overestimating the likely returns, and underestimating the risks.
- Thinking phony diversification alone will protect your investments. If all your funds are betting on shares rising, you aren't really diversified.
- Taking too much risk in the hope of magically earning more money.
- Assuming your McMoney mutual funds are managing all your risks, when they aren't.
- Chasing recent performance. If anything, you should lean the other way, as the sectors that have recently outperformed the rest of the market are more likely to underperform subsequently.
- Trying to build your own stock portfolio. Chances that you will do worse than the market are high. Chances you will do better: slim. Chances you will do a lot better: very slim.
- Owning shares in your employer. This is the riskiest stock to own: Your job already constitutes a sizable investment in the company.
- Keeping all your money in bonds. They aren't a magic bullet any more than stocks are. They are especially at risk from inflation.

- Keeping all your money in the bank. Cash is usually a poor long-term investment. You're taking a big gamble that inflation will stay low.
- Stockpiling gold. It's neither as safe nor as stable as its biggest cheerleaders claim.
- Investing too much in real estate. I hate to be a Monday-morning quarterback, but it is expensive to own, it is hard to buy and sell, and it can decline in price for years.

CHAPTER 5

Storm Proof Your Portfolio

The great secret of the investment world is that nobody actually knows for certain what is going to happen next. (And even those with the best guesses rarely know *when* it will happen.) The wisest professional investors are frequently surprised by events. Economists are wrong so often it has become something of a running joke.

For obvious reasons, Wall Street and those in the finance industry tend not to advertise this too widely. (The furthest they will go is when they advise you to diversify, to protect yourself against different outcomes.)

And once you discover this truth, you may be inclined to panic. If the experts don't know what's going to happen next, how can you possibly invest safely?

Don't despair. The truth can be liberating. The simple answer is to be braced for many eventualities. Don't manage your investments based on what you think is going to happen next. Manage your investments so that you don't care what happens next.

It's not either-or. You don't have to either keep your money in a bank account or take enormous risks speculating on stocks. You don't have to cower in the locker room or do a belly flop off the high board.

If you are scared of or nervous about the markets, there are much easier ways to ease yourself back into the pool. There are perfectly good alternatives within reach of anyone that should give you good returns with lower risk, and let you sleep easily.

In this chapter, we look at investments that can build an all-weather portfolio:

- Inflation-protected government bonds.
- Global index funds.
- Smart, flexible mutual funds that really manage risks.
- Covered call funds.
- Managed precious metals funds.
- Bond funds, including both taxable bonds and municipals.
- Closed-end funds.

We also take a look at three other issues:

1. Timing, or the best way to ease you way into the market.
2. How to handle a stock market crash.
3. How to buy insurance for your company stock (i.e., options).

Inflation-Protected Government Bonds

The U.S. government issues a special type of bond known as Treasury Inflation-Protected Securities (TIPS). They are, in a sense, the safest investments you can buy. They form a great starting point for any portfolio.

Like all other Treasury bonds, TIPS are considered safe from the risk of default. That's because the United States has by far the largest economy in the world and Uncle Sam can always tax it to pay the bills. Perhaps more importantly these days, Uncle Sam also possesses his own Mint, so he is free to print as many dollars as he needs.

But TIPS, unlike other Treasuries, come with a second layer of protection. As their name implies, they also offer a built-in shield

Inflation-Protected Government Bonds

- The safest investment you can buy.
- Issued by the U.S. government.
- Price and coupon secure from default and rising prices.

against rising prices. Their coupon payments rise to match the official consumer price index (CPI).

There are a variety of very simple mutual funds and exchange-traded funds that will buy these for you. The smartest moves are to buy them in a low-cost fund or to buy individual bonds through a broker.

(Other countries also issue inflation-protected bonds. There are some U.S. funds that invest in these, including State Street Global Advisers' SPDR DB International Government Inflation-Protected Bond exchange-traded fund.)

TIPS are sold with a real, postinflation interest rate: That's how much you'll be paid each year on top of the inflation rate. So if you buy TIPS with a real rate of 2 percent, that's what you are guaranteed for the life of the bond, no matter what happens in the economy. If inflation turns out to be zero percent a year, your TIPS will simply pay you 2 percent interest. If inflation rises to 5 percent, the bonds will pay you 7 percent. If inflation rises to 10 percent, they'll pay 12 percent. The coupon and face value of the bond get reset twice a year, to reflect the latest changes in the CPI.

From 2000 through 2009, TIPS actually did better than the U.S. stock market. (See Figure 5.1.) It was an unusual period. You wouldn't expect that result most of the time.

The advantages are obvious.

You know exactly what you are going to get in real, postinflation terms. You can invest tomorrow and know precisely what you will get back in 10 or 20 years' time. There is no such thing as a riskless investment, but TIPS are as close as you get. The guaranteed rate of return makes it easier to plan for the future.

They're a low-worry investment. You can buy them and forget about it. They are particularly useful for those looking for low risk. That includes those nearing or in retirement. It may also include your daughter's college fund in the last couple of years of high school.

The rate of return, obviously, isn't the highest. You wouldn't put all of your money in TIPS. Those with long time horizons might invest only a small part of their retirement money in them. But they will provide any portfolio with some valuable stability.

There are three caveats regarding TIPS that owners should know about.

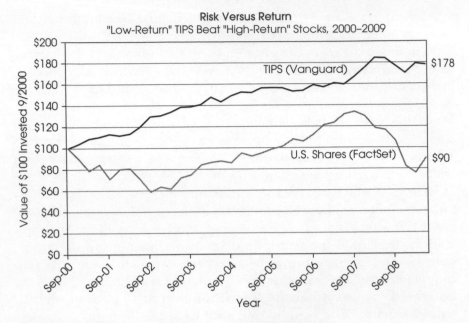

Figure 5.1 TIPS versus Stocks

Data source: Copyright 2009 FactSet Research Systems Inc. All rights reserved.

First, where possible TIPS should always be held in a tax-sheltered account like a 401(k) or an individual retirement account (IRA). That's because these bonds are extremely vulnerable to taxes. The coupons you get twice a year are taxed as ordinary income. But that's not all. The principal is also adjusted in value twice a year to account for any changes in inflation. And that adjustment, too, counts as taxable income even though you won't actually see the money until you sell the bond or it matures.

Second, if consumer prices actually fall—in other words, if the economy enters a period of deflation—the value of a TIPS bond can fall, too. Whether it does, and by how much, is based on complex calculations. This is more likely in theory than in practice. But Japan from the late 1990s has experienced general deflation, so it is not impossible. Note that TIPS will still keep their purchasing power in real terms. (One way to minimize the risk is to buy newly issued TIPS. For technical reasons these will best hold their value. But of course that tends to be reflected in the price. You may find they offer a lower yield.)

Third, not even TIPS can be bought blindly. They are a better deal on some occasions than on others. It depends on the real or after-inflation yield you secure when you buy them. And that varies. When TIPS are popular and lots of people are buying them, the after-inflation yield falls and the bonds are less attractive.

As a rough rule of thumb, TIPS are a poor deal when the real yield falls below 2 percent. When that happens you may be better off waiting to buy more. The U.S. Treasury publishes the real yield every day at www.ustreas.gov/offices/domestic-finance/debt-management/interest-rate/real_yield.shtml.

For a brief period in early 2008, the real yield on TIPS fell to nearly zero. In other words, people buying the bonds at that moment were locking in little or no after-inflation return for the life of the bond. It was a very foolish investment. When I pointed this out in the *Wall Street Journal,* various portfolio managers angrily defended themselves. Their silly defense was that they felt they had to buy something for their clients, then and there, to protect against inflation and this was it.

It made no sense. If something is a poor value, don't buy it. Wait for a better opportunity. With TIPS, such an opportunity unfolded dramatically nine months later. In the depths of the financial crisis various big institutions needed to raise cash immediately. Their TIPS were among the few holdings they could still sell during the panic. So they dumped them all in a rush. Some bonds were sold so cheaply you could get bonds with real yields of 3.5 percent and even 4 percent. It was a slam dunk.

With TIPS, a real yield over 2.5 percent is very good, and 3 percent, if you can get it, is excellent. Longer-term TIPS frequently offer higher yields. The longest-term TIPS are 20-year bonds.

TIPS payments are determined using the official inflation figures, the consumer price index. Some serious economists argue that the CPI understates the true cost of living. If they are right, the real return on TIPS will be less than it appears. It's another argument for trying to get them as cheaply as possible.

Global Index Funds

Everybody now knows the risks of the stock market. But that doesn't mean you should give up on it completely. Shares have produced superior long-term returns in the past, and the cheaper they are, the more likely they are to do so again. The simplest way to capture these potential gains is to set aside part of your portfolio for a pure equities strategy, and to put that money into simple low-cost index funds. But it's worth looking beyond the United States. You can pick either a global index fund or a collection of index funds that follow various international indexes.

Why an Index Fund?

Index funds are the way to keep your costs low. As long as a mutual fund—any mutual fund—has to be fully invested in the stock market at all times, it is probably not going to beat the index over time anyway. So saving on fees makes a lot of sense.

How much do these fees matter? You might be surprised. Imagine three friends—we'll call them Larry, Moe, and Curly. Each one invests $10,000 in the stock market through a mutual fund. Larry buys a fund with a 5 percent front load, or sales charge, and annual expenses of 1 percent a year. Moe buys a fund with no load, but annual expenses of 1.5 percent a year. These two options are pretty typical. And Curly buys an index fund with no sales charge and annual expenses of just 0.2 percent a year.

Let's assume the stock market over the next 20 years proves to be a wonderful place to have your money, gaining 10 percent a year on average. And let's further assume that all three of these funds pick the same stocks and do just as well as each other over that time. The only difference among them is the fees.

Net result? Moe will end up making $41,100 in investment profits from his high-cost fund. Larry will make slightly more: about $43,000.

And Curly? His fund invests no more successfully than those of his friends. But those low fees will really make a difference. His investment profits will come to far more—nearly $55,000.

But that's only half the problem.

What happens if the stock market produces lower returns of, say, 5 percent a year?

The differences are much bigger. This is when those fees really start to hurt.

After 20 years at 5 percent, Moe's fund will make him about $10,000 in profits and Larry's fund will make him nearly $11,000.

Curly's gains? About $15,500 in profits—or about a third higher than his friends' gains.

Why Global?

Most investors tend to stick to their own country's stock market. It's something they know. It feels safe. In the case of the United States, it's also the biggest and most liquid market in the world.

But it's a mistake—especially now. The home market may feel safe, but it's actually pretty risky. Investing globally makes a lot more sense.

You already have some big bets on the U.S. economy. You have your home here. You have your job here. For that matter, so do most of your friends and family. It's crazy the way investors double up by betting on their own country's stock market, too.

Some financial advisers and commentators make matters worse. They pander to this domestic bias, telling investors that international stock markets are much riskier than the U.S. market and more suitable for what they call more aggressive investors. It's a dubious argument.

Investing globally spreads your risks. It allows you to diversify across as many countries, economies, and regions as you can.

Global Index Funds

- Invests in U.S. and overseas stock markets.
- Gives maximum diversification.
- Keeps costs down.

No one knows which countries or regions are going to do best and which will do worst in the years ahead. If you have all your money bet on a single stock market and a single economy, you run the risk of suffering deep losses even while some other markets—perhaps in Asia, perhaps in Europe—do better.

Investing and the Economy

How much attention should investors pay to the economy?

Maybe not as much as some people think.

The real value of your shares lies in the dividends they are going to generate many years, even decades, down the road. The next year (or two) actually has surprisingly little effect. Ben Inker, the director of asset allocation at elite fund management firm Grantham Mayo Van Otterloo, ran the numbers. If you assume that half the return from stocks comes from the dividends and half from the growth of those dividends over time, he said, then:

- Only 25 percent of the value of your shares is actually due to the dividends they are going to generate in the next 11 years.
- Only half the value is from the dividends they are to pay out in the next 25 years.
- A quarter of the value actually comes from the dividends they will generate more than 50 years into the future! So how much do next quarter's earnings really matter?

Source: B. Inker, "Valuing Equities in an Economic Crisis" (GMO research paper, April 2009).

Consider the lessons of history. Those who invested solely in Wall Street before the crash of 1929 lost 89 percent of their money before the market hit rock bottom. And they were sitting on red ink for years. But those who spread their bets internationally—a rare and difficult strategy at the time—fared far better. According to Global Financial Data, Inc., European markets fell a more modest 63 percent and London only about half from peak to trough. That pales against the carnage suffered by investors who had all their money in New York. Global investors were in much better shape throughout the Great Depression.

And consider the fate of investors in Tokyo who stuck to the home market following the 1989 bubble. They suffered a double whammy. The Nikkei fell by more than three-quarters. Meanwhile they missed the boom in the rest of the world. (See Figure 5.2.)

A study in 2006 by the Boston College Center for Retirement Studies found that over the past 80 years those saving in pension

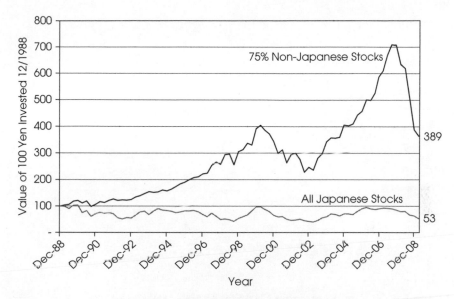

Figure 5.2   How Global Investing Could Have Saved a Japanese Investor
Data source: Copyright 2009 FactSet Research Systems Inc. All rights reserved.

plans would have improved their average returns by investing some of the money overseas.

And that was during the so-called American century, when the United States was by far the biggest and most stable economy in the world. Yet that was an unusual moment in history. Normality has reasserted itself. You now have wide choices, from established economies in Europe to emerging markets in Asia and Latin America. There is no longer any need to rely on just the U.S. economy.

In the past it was hard for ordinary investors to put their money into foreign stock markets. Not anymore. Most good mutual fund companies offer global or world funds. These invest in both the U.S. and foreign stock markets. A single global fund is okay as a one-decision fund if you want to keep things as simple as possible.

But you can probably do better with very little effort. The reason? Most of these global funds still invest too much money in the U.S. market and not enough overseas. They often put about 45 percent or so into U.S. shares, even though the United States now accounts for a lot smaller percentage than that of the world

Figure 5.3   U.S. and Emerging Markets' Shares of World Gross Domestic Product

Data source: International Monetary Fund.

economy. One side effect is that these funds don't put that much into so-called emerging markets like China, Russia, India, and Brazil, even though these have been growing in importance rapidly.

You can see the issue here. Figure 5.3 shows the shares of the world economy accounted for by the United States and by emerging markets. The lines crossed in 2007.

There's a good chance emerging markets will continue to grow faster than more developed countries. But even if they do, that doesn't necessarily mean investors there will do better. That will depend on many other factors, including the price you pay for the shares in the first place. The simplest approach is to adopt a neutral stance. Don't bet on one region (or country) or another. Instead, spread your money evenly across the major parts of the world economy.

First, divide the world into three major blocs: the United States, other developed markets such as Japan and Western Europe, and emerging markets.

Figure 5.4   Shares of the World Economy
Data source: International Monetary Fund.

Second, select low-cost index funds or exchange-traded funds that invest in each one. For example, the Vanguard Total Stock Market index fund invests in the U.S. stock market. The iShares MSCI Europe, Australasia, and Far East (EAFE) index exchange-traded fund invests in developed markets. And the iShares MSCI Emerging Markets Index fund, as the name suggests, invests in developing markets in Asia, Latin America, and elsewhere.

Third, allocate your pure equities investment money across the three blocs in line with their respective shares of the world economy. You can see their respective shares in Figure 5.4. If in doubt, allocating roughly a third to each one will do okay.

Flexible Funds

Not all mutual funds are created equal. Not every fund is run by the marketing department. Not every manager is lashed to a benchmark, or forced to stay fully invested at all times. Some are actually given a free hand and are allowed to manage risk. They can often hold cash if they think shares are overvalued. They can invest in bonds as well as shares if they see value. They may be able to invest in other asset classes, too, including precious metals, convertible securities, derivatives, and the like.

In many cases they can also bet on shares falling as well as rising, using derivatives or a technique known as short selling. It is remarkable how rare this is, or how many people wrongly think it is somehow excessively risky. In professional hands it need be no riskier than betting a share will rise.

The argument for flexibility is obvious and powerful. Markets move. Assets rise and fall in value. Opportunities and dangers arise in different places all the time.

Such flexible, smart funds, of course, are only as good as their managers. And successful investing is an art as well as a science. So there is no automatic system for success. (But if it weren't difficult to find good funds, they couldn't succeed. No investment strategy that can be replicated easily can ever outperform.)

Oddly enough, the whole area of these flexible funds gets a lot less attention than all the inflexible ones out there. That is, in part, because they are difficult to understand and to explain. It's also because they can't be replicated easily, so they don't fit into the McMoney business model. It may also be because, after two decades of a raging bull market, the public wasn't interested in funds that acted more cautiously.

It is a challenge to find the best flexible funds. We'll look later at research sources. It is considerably easier than finding a good private portfolio manager.

These are a small but growing part of the fund management business. There isn't even an established way of categorizing them. Sometimes they get called "market neutral" or "conservative allocation" or "flexible portfolio," and sometimes they are still called "growth" or "value," like many inflexible funds. Sometimes it's hard to know what exactly you are getting. The area isn't clearly defined. But there are at least three main styles, although there is a fair amount of overlap among them (as shown in Figure 5.5):

1. Asset allocation
2. Long-short
3. Maverick

Let's look at each of these in turn.

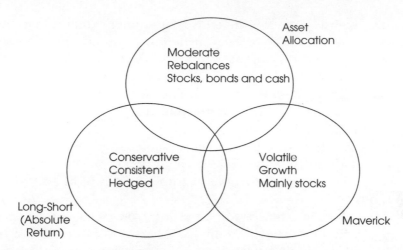

Figure 5.5   Flexible Fund Styles

Asset Allocation Funds

Asset allocation funds spread your money across a broad mix of stocks and bonds. They were designed as a one-stop shop for investors who wanted to pass these decisions on to professionals. Well-known examples include Vanguard Asset Allocation, BlackRock Global Allocation, and Leuthold Asset Allocation. These are designed as conservative investment options.

An asset allocation fund is flexible. When the managers think shares are expensive and bonds are cheap, they will sell some of their shares and buy bonds. And vice versa. A proper asset allocation fund will vary the mix as it goes along, in response to market events.

Asset Allocation Funds

- Shifts key strategic investment decisions to the fund manager.
- Can hold stocks, bonds, and cash.
- Can switch in response to markets.

The managers are actually allowed to manage risk. And they are given a freer hand than most to pursue investment opportunities where they see them, in different asset classes and regions. That's appealing.

The disadvantages? These funds have some flexibility, but sometimes they have too much. They are often required to stick within certain parameters, so they have to hold a certain amount of stocks at all times and a certain amount of bonds. There may be limits to the amount they can invest overseas. They usually can't go short and bet on falling shares, either. And if they are run by big fund companies, they may still be vulnerable to the marketing departments. That may interfere with the managers' game. Many of them still got hit pretty badly in 2007 and 2008.

Figure 5.6 illustrates the potential ups and downs of asset allocation funds.

Asset allocation funds are different from so-called balanced funds. Those, too, invest in a mix of stocks and bonds. But a balanced fund generally keeps the mix unchanged—usually 60 percent stocks, 40 percent bonds. That's really not much different from putting 60 percent of your money in a stock index fund and 40 percent in a bond index fund.

Long-Short Funds

The next category of smart, flexible funds goes one step further. Like a traditional asset allocation fund, long-short funds can move their money around among stocks, bonds, and sometimes other assets like commodities and currencies.

But long-short funds have one further advantage: They can bet on asset prices falling as well as rising. They may buy (or "go long") some stocks and bonds and bet against (or "go short") others. It often also means using derivatives, such as futures and options, to protect against market exposure. Far from being risky, such derivatives can help minimize risk.

These types of funds come under a variety of names. Some are called "absolute return." Others are called "market neutral." Yet others are called "total return." They can differ a great deal in what they do and how they do it.

What they have in common: They typically aim to produce good returns regardless of market conditions. They aren't trying to do well relative to a benchmark, or to the stock market. They are trying to do well in absolute terms—in other words, to make money, and not to lose it.

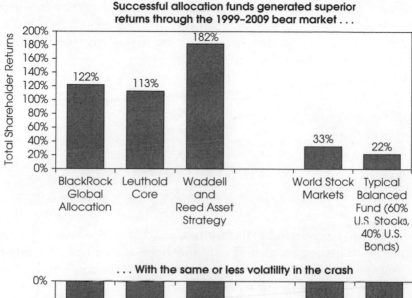

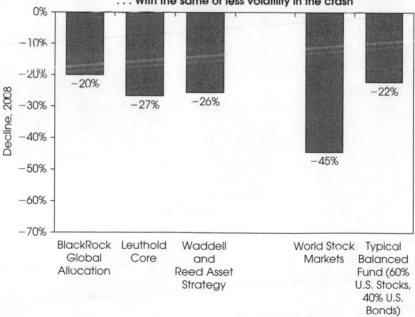

Figure 5.6   Asset Allocation Funds Performance

Data source: Copyright 2009 FactSet Research Systems Inc. All rights reserved.

Some people argue that long-short funds are necessarily a gimmick. It's nonsense. If it is okay for a fund manager to bet that an undervalued share will rise, how can it be wrong for him or her to bet that an overvalued share will fall?

Long-Short Funds

- Tries to produce steadier returns in all markets.
- Has maximum flexibility.
- Can bet on shares falling as well as rising.

After two decades of a roaring bull market, it was maybe understandable that so many would come to believe that the only way to bet on shares is up. But it doesn't make logical sense. Shares are overvalued much of the time.

Many long-short funds tend to put a premium on capital preservation. In other words, making money tends to be their second goal. Their first is not to lose it. Beyond that, though, they vary enormously.

One example is John Hussman's Strategic Growth fund, which has posted pretty steady gains since its launch in 2000. Mr. Hussman, who successfully anticipated much of the financial crisis, was happy to underperform the boom from 2004 to 2007, and then avoided the crash in 2008. Another example is Federated Market Opportunity, run by Steve Lehman and Dana Meissner. Figure 5.7 shows the performance of both, along with a third, Steven Romick's FPA Crescent fund.

The long-short category is relatively new, and it's changing fast.

Many of the big fund companies launched their own products, often with an "absolute return" label, around the time of the financial crisis and its aftermath. It was an obvious marketing opportunity. Ordinary investors were reeling from the turmoil and were looking for stability.

Many of these funds offered the hope of a certain return, such as 4 percent above inflation per year, over the course of a market cycle. And the firms behind them argue they have achieved something

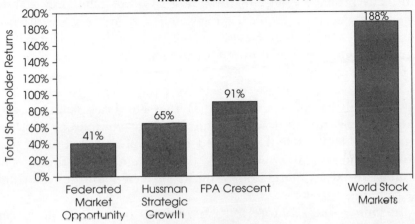

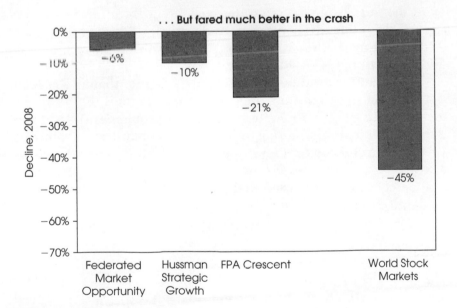

Figure 5.7 Long-Short Funds Performance

Data source: Copyright 2009 FactSet Research Systems Inc. All rights reserved.

similar in the recent past, in funds they have run for big institutions. The problem: Many of these mutual funds have only a short track record, so it's difficult to judge them yet. And it's worth being skeptical of any strategy based on recent historical performance. Remember successful investing is an art as well as a science. There is no philosopher's stone.

Some long-short funds operate in a tiny niche. In early 2009 I interviewed the managers of the Merger Fund, a small, specialist fund that bets up or down on the shares of companies involved in takeover deals. It had produced remarkably good returns over 20 years, and was independent of the stock market indexes. The Merger Fund fell a mere 2 percent in 2008, when almost everything else plummeted.

Including one or more long-short funds in your portfolio can add real value.

If the fund is pursuing a different strategy from others, then it can offer genuine diversification. And while it is likely to underperform a bull market on Wall Street, it will probably do better than the market if shares go sideways or down.

Note that fees for these funds tend to be higher than in a regular stock market fund. And of course fees are important. But don't let them be your only consideration. The main problem with high fees is that most McMoney mutual funds charge them without delivering anything in return except lower performance. But as investors have discovered recently, fees are not the only issue. If a fund avoided a 30 percent loss in the crisis, a 2 percent annual fee seemed like a small price to pay.

Mavericks

The only way to get different results from everybody else is to do something different from them. And that's the specialty of maverick fund managers. These are idiosyncratic investors who are willing to ignore what the rest of the market is doing and pursue their own convictions instead. It takes brains, steady nerves, and a lot of self-confidence.

Like Oscar Wilde at New York Customs, these managers have nothing to declare but their genius.

Successful mavericks include some of the best-known names in the business: people like Warren Buffett, the world's second-richest man, and Ken Heebner and Bill Miller and Marty Whitman and Bob Rodriguez. In Figure 5.8 you can see how some of them have fared.

Someone who backed Warren Buffett when he first began investing in the mid-1950s and stuck with him would have turned

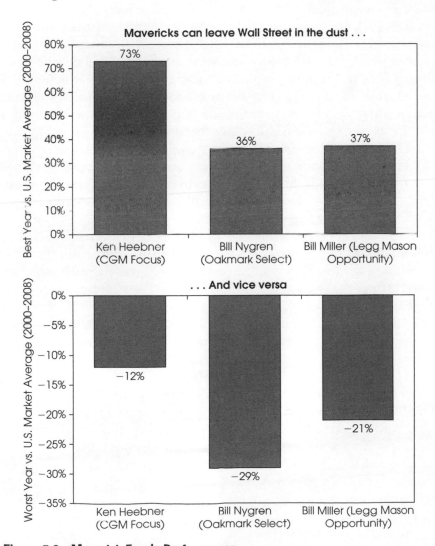

Figure 5.8 Maverick Funds Performance

Data source: Copyright 2009 FactSet Research Systems Inc. All rights reserved.

a $10,000 investment into more than $200 million. In the 15 years from 1990 through 2005, a Wall Street index fund grew a $100 investment into about $500. But over the same period, Bill Miller at Legg Mason Value Trust would have grown it into about $770 and Bob Rodriguez at FPA Capital into nearly $1,100. From 1997 through 2007, while Wall Street barely doubled, Ken Heebner at CGM Focus produced a return of about 800 percent.

Maverick funds can make a great addition to a portfolio. But investors need to understand what they are getting—and what they getting into. Mavericks are very different from typical long-short funds (even though some of them have a limited ability to go short). Instead of producing steady returns in all markets, they may boom miraculously while everyone else is struggling—and then plunge alarmingly when the rest of the market is up.

They are the Tabasco of an investment portfolio. Add sparingly.

This is where so many investors go wrong. When a maverick has just had a good run, he or she typically starts getting lots of attention. New investors jump on the bandwagon. Alas, the manager often then hits a bad patch. Maybe it's because of the pressure of investing all that new money. Or maybe it's because they started to believe their own hype. For whatever reason, when the performance takes a dive, the same investors who jumped on board late jump off again.

Consider the fate of Ken Heebner, the super-maverick who runs CGM Focus fund. He has an excellent long-term record, and has made some of his biggest money as a contrarian, going against the crowd.

By early summer of 2008, while the rest of Wall Street was struggling, he had done so well he was featured on the cover of *Fortune*. The business magazine called him "America's hottest investor," and "the best mutual fund manager around." I'm still kicking myself for not writing what was, in retrospect, an obvious story: "Warning, danger ahead." And so it proved. Mr. Heebner's fund promptly fell flat on its face. He took big bets that the economy was about to rebound—just before Lehman Brothers collapsed and Wall Street crashed.

Others have suffered similar fates. Bill Miller at Legg Mason became a legend for beating Wall Street year after year through the 1990s and into the new millennium. Once the legend became firmly established, he started doing badly. He got pummeled in the financial crisis of 2007 to 2008. First he moved far too early into home-building stocks. Then he bet heavily on Fannie Mae, the federal housing giant, which ended up in bankruptcy.

It happens even to the best of them. The usual public reaction is depressing. Fund managers have been built up too high when they have done well. Then they get torn down when they do badly.

The better response: Understand what you own, and treat it accordingly. Be careful with maverick funds. It's a needless risk to put too much faith, or money, with one individual. Do not be captivated by dreams that one magical genius is going to make you rich. The usual rule about holy grails always applies.

Maverick Funds

- Run by an idiosyncratic manager.
- Ignores benchmarks.
- Apt to be volatile.

By definition, a maverick's performance will be quirky. Even Warren Buffett saw his share price halve in the late 1990s, while much of the market soared. Many people will invest with individuals in the hope that they will do something different from the overall market, and are then shocked, or horrified, when they do exactly that.

If they never underperform, they can never outperform. It's as simple as that.

How to Use Smart Funds

You need to understand what you are buying. A good long-short fund is likely to steady your portfolio but may slow it down. A maverick fund may do the reverse. There is no reason at all to stick with only one smart fund, or even only one style.

Be aware there can be plenty of overlap, too. So, for example, many maverick funds can go short as well as long. It takes on more risk.

How do you go about finding out more about intelligent, flexible mutual funds? Here are several resources.

- *Morningstar*, the Chicago-based company that analyzes mutual funds (www.morningstar.com). Morningstar publishes detailed reports on individual funds. These can help you understand the strengths and risks of individual fund managers and various funds, their past records, and their strategies.
- *The fund manager's own web site.* The company should offer its own pretty detailed take on what the fund does and how it operates. Performance figures are subject to U.S. regulations. The fund managers' quarterly reports to shareholders usually offer great insight into what they do and how they operate. Those who admit to their mistakes candidly deserve credit. Those who try to pin all the blame on outside events don't.
- *Online financial sites*, including those of the *Wall Street Journal* (www.wsj.com), MarketWatch (www.marketwatch.com), Bloomberg (www.bloomberg.com), TheStreet.com (www.thestreet.com), Reuters (www.reuters.com), SeekingAlpha (www.seekingalpha .com) and Yahoo! Finance (http://finance.yahoo.com). It's worth reading around the topic to see what others are saying about a fund. It's also worth looking at performance charts to see how the fund has done over time.
- *Advisers.* A good financial adviser may be able to offer insights and guidance regarding individual funds. The problem? Finding a good adviser is even harder than finding good smart funds. And it's harder to check their performance, too. Too many people choose advisers based on charm, personality, and referrals from friends who aren't experts, either.

Here are some things to look for in choosing smart funds:

- *Strategies that are genuinely different from just owning shares.* If the performance chart just looks like the stock market, it's not going to give you something different.
- *Gray hairs.* Investment managers tend to get better as they get older. Often they don't enter their prime until they are in their fifties—and have seen at least one bear market. (Happily, there are now many more managers around who have been tested by a bear market.) Time also helps weed out crooks and fools.
- *A long-term track record.* Ideally that means at least a decade. Anyone can do well, or badly, for a few years. That alone doesn't mean much. And look at how they fared during the crash. But be aware that almost everybody did badly for a few months. That alone doesn't show much.
- *Clear communications.* Be wary of a fund manager who cannot explain his or her strategy, or recent events, in plain language. Most of the time, clear language is a sign of clear thinking. Jargon is not a sign of wisdom.
- *Fund size.* Big funds find it much harder to dance. Few managers can outperform for long periods of time with much more than $10 billion or so. The smaller, usually, the better.
- *An independent firm.* The best fund managers often work for their own company. That leaves them free to do what they think is right. Big companies are the death of independent thinking. They strangle it with endless meetings and quarterly reviews and red tape and marketing requirements and peer pressure and office politics.
- *Diversification.* If you own more than one smart fund, you minimize your exposure to any individual strategy or manager.

You don't have to go any further to build a storm proofed portfolio. Treasury Inflation-Protected Securities (TIPS) will give you stability. A low-cost global equity fund or funds will give you the maximum exposure to any gains on global stock markets. And some flexible smart funds will give your portfolio the ability to adapt to circumstances as they arise.

But you can add other strategies and investments to spread your bets still further.

The main extra alternatives I'll look at here are covered call funds, precious metals funds, taxable and municipal bonds, and closed-end funds.

Covered Call Funds

A covered call fund, also known as a buy-write fund, can put stabilizers on a portfolio without necessarily slowing you down too much.

These pursue an unusual strategy. They buy shares, much like any other fund, and then generate steady profits by selling derivatives against those shares. In layperson's terms they are betting that the shares won't rise very far in the month or months ahead. This strategy is less arcane or dangerous than it may sound. It has a record of producing solid returns in most environments. Investors give up the chance of big short-term gains. But the sale of derivatives generates pretty good cash flow instead.

These funds tend to lag a simple index fund during a bull market, for obvious reasons: You're giving up some of your profits when shares boom. On the other hand, these funds tend to handsomely outperform index funds in flat or falling markets.

The most detailed study of this strategy was conducted in 2006 by Callan Associates, an investment services consulting company, on behalf of the Chicago Board Options Exchange. They looked at how a mainstream covered call strategy, based on the Standard & Poor's 500 stock index, would have performed if you had pursued it consistently from as far back as 1988.

Their conclusions (shown in Figure 5.9) were remarkable. Over 18 years, they said, the strategy would have actually made you about the same amount as simply holding a stock market index fund—but would have done so with about one-third less volatility. It even had less volatility than the Lehman Brothers bond index, while making much more money.

One of the better-known examples of a covered call fund is the Gateway Fund. From 1998 through 2008, while shares did so badly, it gained about 40 percent. And it fell far less than the stock market during the big slumps of 2000 to 2002 and 2007 to 2009. (Gateway

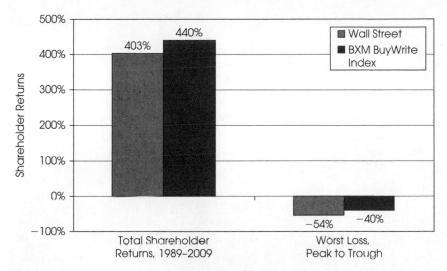

Figure 5.9 BXM BuyWrite Index Beat Wall Street over 20 Years—with Less Volatility

is more conservative than most other covered call funds. During the bull market that preceded these slumps it produced lower returns than shares.)

A covered call strategy is the kind of investment option that got very little attention during the last bull market, but which investors should consider much more closely now. There are now many mutual funds, exchange-traded funds, and closed-end funds (more about those later) that pursue this strategy. There is, of course, no guarantee a covered call fund will produce superior returns. But including it within your portfolio has a decent chance of steadying the ship.

Covered Call Funds

- Specialist strategy.
- Sells call options against shares.
- Can produce good returns with lower volatility.
- Reinvest the dividends to get the full long-term performance.

Precious Metals

In Chapter 4 I explained why the more hysterical and paranoid arguments for gold should be taken with a grain of another product that's been valued for about 3,000 years—salt.

But that doesn't mean you have to leave precious metals—including gold, platinum, and silver—alone altogether.

There are actually solid investment reasons why you might want to have some exposure to precious metals in your portfolio. And there is a smarter, more sensible way to do it than burying gold coins in your backyard.

Governments around the world have been printing dollars, yen, euros, pounds, francs, and other paper currencies at a record pace. This has gone on for years, but in the financial crisis of 2007 to 2009 it speeded up. The laws of supply and demand are not complex. When you vastly increase the supply of something, the price tends to fall. When you create a lot more of something the price generally declines. That's true of MP3 players, Las Vegas condos, and dollars.

Americans face two more problems that may further undermine the strength of the dollar.

First, the U.S. government has been running a gigantic budget deficit almost every year for a generation. The national debt, which was less than $1 trillion as recently as 1980, is now forecast to pass $14 trillion in 2010. The scale of the borrowing is without precedent in peacetime. (See Figure 5.10.)

And second, even more alarmingly, the United States as a country has been running a huge deficit with the rest of the world. (See Figure 5.11.)

When you put all that together you get a dangerous fact: The American economy, as well as the U.S. federal budget, depends on the kindness of strangers. The world's biggest economy must borrow billions of dollars a week from abroad just to pay its bills.

Figure 5.12 shows the value of U.S. Treasury bonds owned by overseas investors.

This can hardly continue indefinitely. And it raises risks for the dollar.

It would be tempting to seek refuge in other currencies. Most of them have been going through a similar process. Governments

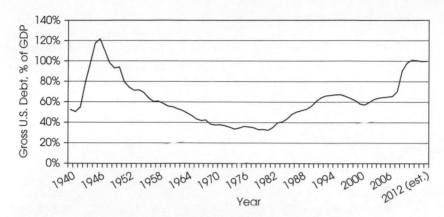

Figure 5.10   Federal Government Debt as a Share of the Economy
Data source: White House budget documents, historical tables.

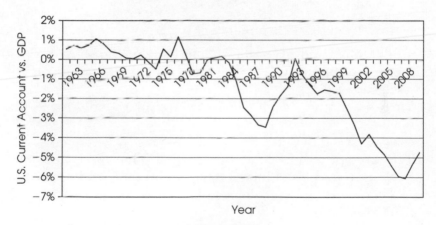

**Figure 5.11   U.S. Current Account Balance as a Percentage of
Gross Domestic Product**
Data source: BEA/Commerce Department, White House budget documents.

around the world have also been running big deficits and flooding
their economies with new money.

A fund manager I know jokes that currencies these days are like
political parties. You end up choosing the one you dislike the least.

This should be positive news for anything of limited supply
and reasonably constant demand. Gold, along with other precious

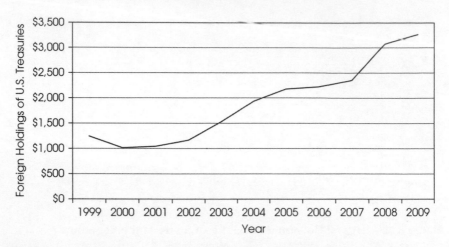

Figure 5.12   U.S. Government's Foreign Debt ($ Billions)
Data source: U.S. Treasury International Capital (TIC) data.

metals like silver and platinum, should benefit. (So should ocean-front property, but my global warming pals tell me it's all going to be washed away. Pity.)

There is another benefit to including some exposure to precious metals.

They behave differently from other assets.

They are apt to do well at a time when other assets are suffering, such as in periods of high inflation. And they tend to perform poorly when other assets are doing well, such as during a low-inflation boom like the 1990s.

Precious Metals Funds

- Specialist strategy.
- Can own metals and shares in mining companies.
- May protect against inflation and decline in the dollar.

Some investors have been buying gold bullion or coins. Others have been pouring money into bullion funds, like the SPDR Gold Trust, which are backed by gold held in bank vaults. But these are

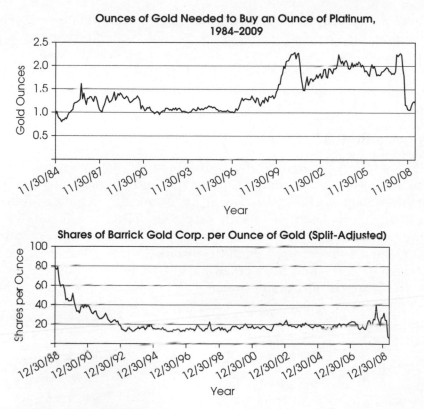

Figure 5.13 Two Gold Charts

Data source: Copyright 2009 FactSet Research Systems Inc. All rights reserved.

not the only gold options. Investors may be better off over time, and sleep more easily, if they choose a third option: a managed fund that can buy gold, other metals, or the shares of gold mining companies. Examples include Fidelity Select Gold and Tocqueville Gold.

Sometimes the best opportunities may lie in holding the metals directly. At other times they may lie in mining stocks—whether big, established companies or more speculative miners. At different times gold may be expensive and platinum and silver may be better values, or vice versa. Smart managers have shifted out of one and into another. (See Figure 5.13.) At other times shares in big mining companies have been cheap in relation to the metal, or expensive.

There have frequently been opportunities—and pitfalls—among smaller, more speculative mining companies. And of course mining companies, unlike metal bars, generate income for shareholders.

A managed precious metals fund, unlike a direct holding in gold, may give you some exposure to precious metals without the white-knuckle risks of holding gold directly.

Taxable Bonds

Bonds are IOUs. They can be issued by institutions ranging from Uncle Sam to a small company. They can make a good addition to an investment portfolio. But the bond universe is complex—more so than shares. There are plenty of pitfalls. There are many different types of bonds, both U.S. and foreign, government, and private. Corporate bonds vary from high yield to investment grade. Preferred stock, despite its name, is effectively a bond. Convertible bonds, which can be swapped into shares in some circumstances, are a specialist investment area on their own. Each type of bond offers a different mix of potential returns and risks.

Taxable Bonds

- An IOU issued by a company or government.
- In most cases you get a series of interest payments and your principal back at the end.
- Long-term bonds are at greater risk from inflation.

The risks posed by bonds are inflation, default, taxes, exchange rate, and complexity.

- *Inflation.* You wouldn't want to buy a bond guaranteeing you 4 percent a year for 30 years shortly before inflation rose to 8 percent and bank rates to 10 percent. If that happened, the price of your bond would fall and the purchasing power of your money would be eroded over time. Long-term bonds involve much more inflation risk than short-term ones, though they usually offer higher interest rates to compensate.
- *Default.* Bonds issued by individual companies can default if the company goes bankrupt. Bondholders may get back

little or nothing of their original stakes. This risk is mostly
confined to corporate bonds. But occasionally bonds issued
by some municipal authorities, or by overseas governments,
threaten default as well. High-yield bonds have a greater risk
of default than investment-grade bonds.

- *Taxes.* Stock dividends get treated generously by the U.S.
tax code. Bond coupons don't. They get taxed at ordinary
income tax rates. By raising your taxable income, they may
also raise the danger that retirees will be taxed on their Social
Security income. The one exception: municipal bonds, which
are exempt from federal income tax and usually from taxa-
tion within the state of issue.

- *Exchange rate.* Investors have become more willing in recent
years to invest in bonds issued by overseas corporations and
governments. The returns they get will be affected by the
exchange rate. If you buy a bond issued in euros and the euro
rises against the dollar, your bond and your coupons are
worth more in the United States. But if the euro falls, they
are worth less. Overseas bonds, understandably, attract investors who think the dollar is going to fall.

- *Complexity.* Bonds vary a lot more than shares. They range
from short-term Treasury bonds, which are ultrasafe, to com-
plicated and risky corporate paper. Many investors lost money
in the summer of 2008 on so-called convertible preferreds, a
sort of bond issued by Fannie Mae and Freddie Mac. Many
advisers assured their clients these were safe and conservative
investments. They weren't.

Some people buy their own bonds directly. In the case of Treasury
or municipal bonds, this can make sense. You keep the costs low and
you can structure when you receive interest payments. But it's a fair
amount of work and you need to do your homework. And in the
case of corporate bonds it can involve a lot of risk. Companies, even
well-known ones, can end up in bankruptcy. When that happens, the
bondholders may get as little back as the stockholders: nothing.

You may hear a lot of simplistic rules about bonds. Like most simplistic investment rules, they don't withstand serious investigation.

*Are bonds issued by foreign governments riskier than those issued in
the United States?* Some foreign countries, such as Switzerland and

What's in a Yield?

If you are going to buy individual bonds, you had better know the yield, or interest rate, you will get. But it's not that simple. Each bond can have as many as five different yields. This is the kind of jargon that puts most people off. Which yield is which? And which one matters?

1. *Coupon yield.* This is the interest rate on the label of the bond ("Amalgamated Widgets 6%," and so on). But look out: it's probably not the interest rate you will get, unless you bought the bond the day it was issued. The coupon yield is simply the value of the annual coupons divided by the issue price (or face value) of the bond. Bonds rarely trade for exactly the face value.

2. *Current yield.* This is the annual interest rate you will get from the bond's coupons. But, once again, it's not the full return most people will get. The problem? It ignores any capital gain, or loss, you will make when you sell the bond or it matures. If you buy a bond for $1,200 and you get back only $1,000 when it matures, you will need to factor that $200 loss into your total returns. Current yield won't tell you.

3. *Yield to maturity.* This is a more useful number. It's the annual return you will get if you buy a bond today and hold it until it matures. It counts what you pay for the bond, the coupons you will get each year, and any capital gain or loss at the end. But before you relax, there's a catch: You may not get to hold the bond until maturity. That's because some bonds can be called before they mature. That means the issuer can pay them off early, like a mortgage.

4. *Yield to call.* This tells you how much you will get if the bond is called early. However, it has the reverse problem: The bond might not be called at all. In that case the yield to call will be irrelevant.

5. *Yield to worst.* If you can find out only one yield about a bond, this is it. The yield to worst means the lesser of the yield to maturity or the yield to call. If reading that sentence gives you a headache, just remember: The yield to worst is the actual annual return you'll get if you buy a bond today and hold it for as long as you can.

Denmark, have traditionally been far more fiscally conservative than Washington, D.C. (Others, of course, haven't—Russia defaulted on its debt as recently as 1998.) But the risks investors are taking may also depend on the price they are paying.

Are municipal bonds, issued by cities and states, riskier than Treasuries? Reality: Defaults among high-quality municipal bonds have been almost nonexistent in modern history. Even during the Depression the default rates were minuscule. No state has defaulted on its bonds since before the Civil War. Yet during the 2008 financial crisis many investors dumped their munis in panic. Result? Municipals became an absolute steal. At one point they were paying about twice the interest rate as Treasuries—and their interest payments were tax free. It made no sense.

Are investment-grade corporate bonds always a safer investment than high-yield bonds? Up to a point. But, as ever, price matters. First, whether or not a bond is deemed investment grade relies on the verdict of a few professional rating agencies such as Standard & Poor's, Moody's Investors Service, and Fitch Ratings. They have been known to change their minds about a bond long after it's been issued. Never forget that many of the worthless subprime bonds that were such junk that they nearly brought down the international capitalist system in 2008 began life as investment-grade bonds.

Companies that used to be strong become weak. Circumstances change. Stable industries become turbulent. A bond that begins life legitimately as investment grade, offering little apparent risk of default, may later become riskier.

Individual bonds can default. But any reasonable bond fund buys many bonds issued by many different companies in many different industries. And, barring some extraordinary set of circumstances, they won't all default. As usual, you can't separate price and risk. Even a basket of deeply distressed bonds can prove a bargain if you buy them cheaply enough. If you buy enough unrelated bonds at 30 cents on the dollar, those that end up paying back the full face value may more than compensate you for those that pay nothing. By contrast, supposedly safe bonds may prove a very risky bet if you pay too much.

Are "Junk" Bonds Really Junk?

- So-called high-yield or junk bonds are those issued by companies with a noticeable risk of default. Some are riskier than others.
- They usually pay higher rates of interest to compensate for the risk that they might default.
- While a single junk bond can be very risky, a broad basket of them is less so. Usually only a few will default.
- In an economic crisis, a high-yield or junk bond fund may prove a particularly good investment. That's because junk bonds may be selling so cheaply that those that do pay out may more than compensate you for those that default.

Those looking for a simpler life can look at bond funds instead. There are two main kinds:

1. *Sector funds.* There's a wide range that will give you exposure to almost any type of bond you want. You can buy shares in a California municipal bond fund or a long-term Treasury fund or a high-yield fund. Index funds will spread your bets across the sector. They generally have low fees. Others will charge you more but will attempt to pick the right bonds.
2. *General funds.* These can be great for one-stop shopping. They will buy bonds from across almost all sectors, including Treasuries or corporates. This allows them to capitalize on opportunities throughout the bond world. If you aren't comfortable with bonds, this is the way to go. Well-known general bond funds include Pimco Total Return, run by Bill Gross, and Loomis Sayles Bond, run by Dan Fuss. Note: General funds rarely invest in tax-free municipals.

Municipals

The state of California borrows money. So does the city of Poughkeepsie, New York. When they do, they issue bonds just like anyone else. But there's one big difference. The bonds are tax free.

The interest payments are exempt from federal income tax, as well as taxes in the issuing state.

That's a pretty valuable kicker, especially to anyone in a higher income tax bracket. Someone paying 25 percent income tax would have to earn 10 percent interest in a taxable bond to match the net income he'd get from a 7.5 percent muni. Someone in a 35 percent bracket would have to earn just over 11.5 percent.

We've already looked at why high-grade munis can be a good investment in your emergency fund. But that isn't their only benefit. If you are in a higher income tax bracket, muni bonds can also make sense for other reasons. The yield is often higher than it should be because the market for municipals, especially long-term bonds, is inefficient.

Studies consistently show that some investors hold municipal bond funds in tax shelters like IRAs. It makes no sense. Munis are already tax exempt. Holding them in a tax shelter is a waste of a tax shelter.

Municipal Bonds

- Issued by states, cities, and other municipal authorities.
- Normally exempt from income tax.
- Highest-quality bonds are nearly as secure as Treasuries.

Municipal bonds come in many shapes and sizes. The most secure are known as general obligation bonds, or GOs. They are backed by the "full faith and credit" of the city or state that issues them. This means they'll raise taxes, if they have to, to pay the coupons. These bonds have historically proved incredibly secure. Defaults are almost nonexistent. After all, many of the investors are local residents. Do the politicians really want to default on the interest payments? Almost as good are top-rated municipal bonds backed by the revenues of essential services like water. For obvious reasons these tend to enjoy stable revenue flows. People, to put it bluntly, do not stop going to the bathroom in a recession. Indeed, if the stock market plunges 1,000 points in an afternoon, they may go more.

How secure from default are municipal bonds? A study by Moody's Investors Service, the ratings agency, found that over the past 35 years investment-grade munis have defaulted at paltry rates—about one per 15,000 each year. Excluding the top general obligation and water bonds, the rate was still only about one per 3,500 a year. However, even the most highly rated are not the same as Treasuries. Municipalities can default. Unlike Uncle Sam, they cannot print their own money.

And some municipal bonds are a bit riskier. So-called high-yield municipals may be issued by independent charter schools, nursing homes, local health clinics, even private corporations. That's the case when they use the money for certain local purposes like cleaning up pollution. These types of bonds still don't default that often. They tend to rank alongside pretty good, if not quite top-quality, corporate bonds.

During the panic of 2008 the market got so crazy that municipals actually yielded far more than Treasuries, even before counting the tax benefit. While Uncle Sam was paying 2.6 percent for his money, some states were paying more than twice as much.

Municipals can make an excellent investment, especially for those in or near retirement or in a higher tax bracket. But when you buy anything other than the most secure general obligation bonds, you start to take on risk. It may make more sense to buy them through a fund. One very compelling vehicle for buying munis is a closed-end fund. That's a special type of investment we'll look at next.

Closed-End Funds

Few investors know about closed-end funds. Even fewer really understand them. It's a shame. These can make a terrific addition to your portfolio—if you are willing to do your homework.

Closed-end funds aren't a separate asset class, like shares or bonds or gold. They are just a different type of mutual fund. You invest by buying shares in the fund on the stock market.

What makes them appealing is that you can often get these funds on sale. Shares in a closed-end fund, for unusual, technical reasons, can drop a long way below the value of the investments inside the fund. So even though a fund may hold investments worth $10 a share, you may be able to buy shares in the fund itself for $8.50 or even less. These types of anomalies are particularly common during a market panic, when some investors sell everything.

There were moments, in 2007 and 2008, when many closed-end funds plunged to 80 cents or even 70 cents on the dollar.

If a fund is at a discount when you buy it and it's still on the same discount when you sell it 10 years later, you haven't lost or gained anything. But if you buy it at 80 cents in a time of panic and sell it later for 95 cents when the market has righted itself, you've made a big bonus on top of any underlying investment gain.

Closed-End Funds

- Regulated mutual fund.
- You buy and sell its shares on the stock market like company stocks.
- Shares often sell for 90 cents on the dollar or less.

But the benefits can go further. You can target good closed-end funds that pay high dividends. These might invest in bonds or high-dividend stocks. If you buy shares in the fund when they are on sale, you will get more dividends for each dollar you put in. If you tell your broker to put the fund on a dividend reinvestment plan, each dividend check will be used to buy more shares. Over the long term this can generate good returns.

For this reason, closed-end funds can be great vehicles for investing in bonds. If the fund's shares are trading at a discount, you get more bonds, and therefore more bond coupons, for your investment dollar.

There are pitfalls to avoid. Some closed-end fund discounts are misleading, because the fund could never realize the net asset value. For example, it might have a big tax liability on capital gains if it ever liquidated its investments. Sometimes the dividend yield needs to be treated with caution, too: Many funds have so-called managed distributions and may pay their dividends out of reserves.

This means effectively you are just getting your own money back. You can usually tell if a fund is earning its keep because the underlying net asset value is stable or rising. Think twice before buying shares in a closed-end fund that has high payouts but a constantly falling share price.

And closed-end funds tend to be more volatile than regular mutual funds, because in times of stress the shares can fall a long way below the value of the fund. If you may need your money back in a hurry, or you cannot stand that kind of turmoil, that can be a problem.

Good sources of information include the Closed-End Fund Association, whose web site is at www.cefa.org, and Nuveen Investments, which runs the ETF Connect web site at www.etfconnect.com. These offer lots of data, including the share prices, net asset values, and discounts every day. Thomas J. Herzfeld Advisors, Inc., a boutique investment firm in Miami, specializes in closed-end funds. The best-known companies running closed-end funds are Eaton Vance, Nuveen, and BlackRock.

There are two further issues to look at:

1. Timing, or how to ease yourself back into the market.
2. How best to react to a stock market crash.

Timing: Little and Often

Deciding it's safe to get back in the water is very different from actually taking the plunge.

Timing is a major challenge for investors. You could be forgiven for thinking it's never the right time to get into the market—or to get out. If your shares are down, you don't want to sell them now. Can you just wait until they recover before selling? But of course you don't know if they will recover, or when.

And who wants to get into the stock market just before it crashes? Someone who invested in Wall Street on September 3, 1929, just before the great crash, had to wait more than two decades before the Dow Jones Industrial Average got back to that same level. Instead, over the next three years, the markets plummeted by nearly 90 percent.

For obvious reasons, this will still matter to you most in relation to the equity portion of your portfolio: the part invested in shares, such as a global index fund or funds.

TIPS are not especially volatile: As long as you make sure to buy them when they have a good after-inflation yield, the timing of your purchase is unlikely to matter very much.

Asset allocation and long-short mutual funds take some of the issue out of your hands. Timing is one of the things the fund manager is supposed to handle. If he or she believes the market is dangerously overvalued and at risk of a sharp fall, then the fund may already be positioned defensively.

Other investment options, such as covered call and bond funds, are also less vulnerable to market slumps. They may be affected, but not to the same degree as the stock market.

When it comes to investing in shares, there is a good strategy to minimize any risks.

Keep investing, regularly, month after month. If you save the same amount, it's a process known as dollar-cost averaging. When shares are cheap, you'll get more of them. When they are more expensive, you'll get fewer. It sounds low-tech and unsophisticated, but no one has ever found a better system.

If you put your investments on a dividend reinvestment plan, your dividend checks will automatically be used to buy more units in the fund.

You should be able to set one up through your broker or retirement plan. If you subscribe to a mutual fund directly through the fund company, you should be able to do it through them.

Reinvesting will also smooth your returns over time. It minimizes the danger of getting into the market shortly before a slump.

Waiting instead for the right moment to jump in is almost certainly a waste of time. Nobody knows when the market will hit bottom. No one rings a bell or sounds the all-clear. Maybe March 2009 will prove to be the low this time. But then, many thought that in November 2008. Indeed, many thought it had hit bottom in October 2002. It turned out that was only two years into the bear market.

November 1929, shortly after the great crash of 1929, felt like the low to many. Share prices had fallen about half from their peak. But those who bet everything at once lost their shirts. The market fell around 80 percent more over the following three years. No one thought the summer of 1932 would prove to be the all-time low. But it was.

Only those who simply ignored the moves and kept buying a few shares every month, dollar-cost averaging as they went, eventually did well.

Nothing is perfect. At the time, even these sensible investors had to endure several very tough years. According to stock market returns from Global Financial Data, someone who started dollar-cost averaging at the start of 1929 still lost two-thirds of the investment by the lows in 1932. But by 1936, those who had stayed the course had doubled their money. Those who kept it at for decades became seriously rich.

Dollar-cost averaging goes a long way toward stabilizing your portfolio. But you can help yourself still further by taking a pledge to review your investments, and rebalance them where necessary, at regular intervals—say once every six months or every year. If you are going to review them annually, there is one easy way to remember the date. Just do it around the time of your birthday each year.

This gives you a chance to rein in your exposure to a galloping stock market, or to increase your exposure to one that has fallen a long way. It helps you to set limits and to be disciplined.

In the boom of 2005 to 2007, many people saw the shares in their portfolios boom far ahead of everything else. People who had chosen to have 50 percent of their money in shares found they now had 75 percent. Those who reined that back in, by selling some of their shares and buying more bonds, saved themselves some grief.

But of course one of the advantages of including some flexible, managed funds in your portfolio is that they minimize this risk. The managers will be handling some of these issues.

And if you can't correctly gauge the market bottom with confidence, you can't jump on rallies, either.

Wall Street saw 16 rallies of more than 15 percent between late 1929 and 1946. The market initially jumped by nearly 50 percent immediately after the crash itself, starting in November 1929.

There were three big sucker rallies in 1931, when the market rose by more than a fifth.

Investors must have thought they were witnessing the launch of a new bull market in 1932, when the market soared 77 percent, or in 1933, when it more than doubled. As in Japan, at least one rally lasted years—from 1935 through 1937 the Dow Jones Industrial Average doubled. There were also big booms in 1938, when it rose 59 percent, and 1942–1943, when it jumped 56 percent.

As it happens, the all-time low was seen in 1932, but that didn't help those who jumped on board during a rally. They got crushed when the market collapsed again.

Consider the bear market of Wall Street in the 1970s. From its peak in 1968 to its low in 1982, the market lost value even before counting inflation. In real terms, it fell in value by two-thirds. Yet during that time there were seven big rallies, including three of more than 40 percent.

In the years after 1990, the Japanese stock market saw many big surges. Each time the cheerleading chorus of stockbrokers insisted the bear market was over. Each time bullish sources said the market was heading back up to 39,000, and beyond. Each time nervous investors were told they had better get in now, before it was too late.

If you just count rallies where the market rose at least 15 per cent, Tokyo saw no fewer than 13 during those two decades. And many of them were simply huge: At the time they must surely have seemed like new bull markets, and many investors must have felt, to borrow the phrase from *Jaws II*, that it was "safe to go back in the water."

Between late 1990 and the middle of 1994, the Nikkei witnessed four separate rallies in which it rose by around a third. In 1995–1996 it rocketed up by more than 50 percent. In the late 1990s it boomed by more than 60 percent, and from 2003 through 2006, astonishingly, it more than doubled. Yet after each boom the market collapsed back to fresh lows.

Bottom line: You can never be certain about timing. It's another reason for not taking big bets. Investing little and often helps protect you.

How to Handle a Crash

It is worth remembering: A crisis is often the best time to invest.

Each one feels like the end of the world. Yet somehow the world carries on. No matter how bad things get, they probably won't get anywhere near as bad as the terrible crash in London in the early

1970s. The British stock market fell by about three-quarters, hitting lows last seen 20 years earlier. House prices collapsed. Inflation skyrocketed. It's hard to remember now, but at the time Britain looked like a total basket case. Strikes crippled the economy—at one point so many workers in the power companies were on strike that they reduced the country to a three-day workweek. The socialist government, vowing to "squeeze the rich till the pips squeak," raised taxes to confiscation levels. The country that had once run the Third World now appeared to be joining it. Some even speculated about a possible coup.

At the depths of the crisis, Jim Slater, a prominent financier, warned that the only investments anyone would need would be stocks of canned goods and gold coins, a bicycle, "and a shotgun to protect your family."

The stock market hit bottom shortly afterward, and then promptly started shooting upward. Prosperity returned. Anyone who invested and held on for 10 years made a fortune.

In the crash of 1929 to 1932 Wall Street fell about 90 percent. Ron Chernow, in his book *The House of Morgan* (Atlantic Monthly Press, 1990), writes that business on Wall Street grew so bad that stockbrokers often took the day off to sell apples in the street. And members of the upper-crust Union League Club of New York grew so despondent that they used their worthless share certificates to paper the walls of the library.

It proved the greatest buying opportunity in history. The Dow Jones Industrial Average, which hit a low of 42 in 1932, rose as high as 195 five years later. Union League members had to steam their stock certificates off the library wall.

The crash of 2008 wasn't Wall Street's first crash. It wasn't even the fifth. It was the 18th since 1800. The market crashed in 1812, 1837, 1857, 1873, 1903, 1907, 1914, 1917, 1937, 1946, 1966, 1973–1974, 1976–1978, 1987, 1998, and 2000–2003, as well, of course, as the most famous one of all—the great crash of 1929, which actually went on for four years.

At the time, many of these crashes seemed terrifying. Most have been long forgotten. Henry Clews, a nineteenth-century financier, recalled that some wise men in the Victorian era grew rich simply by keeping their heads when everyone else panicked. These individuals, he remembered, lived easy and comfortable lives on country estates in places like Connecticut. They rarely ventured into New York until there was a stock market panic.

Then they would travel down to Wall Street and buy lots of stocks at fire sale prices. They would wait until the market recovered and prices boomed again, and then sell their shares for an enormous profit. Then they would travel back to Connecticut to relax—until the next panic.

Crashes are the time to buy shares, not to sell them. So many banks and brokerage houses collapsed in the great crash of 1873 that the New York Stock Exchange had to be closed for 10 days. Yet according to Global Financial Data, a firm that tracks historical stock market data, anyone who braved the panic to buy a basket of common stocks trebled their money over the following 20 years. Anyone who did the same during the great panic of 1907 made a 700 percent gain.

Westerners may barely recall it, but those who lived in Southeast Asian countries suffered a terrifying economic collapse in 1997 and 1998. It wasn't just a financial crisis, either. The economies were plunged into turmoil. Some countries saw riots. The situation in Indonesia was so bad that it eventually drove long-standing president Suharto from power.

But anyone who jumped into these stock markets at the depths of the crisis, when the situation was at its worst, made a mint. Hong Kong and Singapore doubled within a year of the lows.

Someone who panics and sells in a crash has not learned the correct lessons. Often people bought their shares when the market was booming and felt safe. Yet, of course, it proved to be nothing of the sort. When the market is booming, shares are usually expensive, and that, paradoxically, makes them risky.

In the stock market, feelings do not equal facts. Natural human instincts can mislead you. There is no safety in numbers. When the market has collapsed and feels most dangerous, shares are much cheaper. That makes them a much safer long-term home for your money. And markets usually start rallying well before signs of recovery in the wider economy. Received wisdom on Wall Street is that the market is about nine months ahead.

One of the most conservative (and successful) money managers I know can usually be found buying during a panic. His rationale: History says that when a market or a particular sector has fallen about 70 percent or so from its peak it is usually a good long-term investment. Those who buy and hold on for about five years, he says, will most of the time beat the market indexes. (Like all things, this involves fine judgment. Some sectors will go to zero.) It's not for the fainthearted.

My favorite advice about crashes comes from the Wall Street classic *Where Are the Customers' Yachts?* by Fred Schwed Jr. He was a stockbroker who had lived through the crash of 1929 and the Great Depression that followed, before writing his financial classic in 1940. His conclusion? When the stock market is booming and everyone wants to get on board, he said, sell all your stocks and put your money in conservative bonds. Wait until the stock market collapses. When it does, and the crisis is shaking the nation, sell all your bonds . . . and buy stocks again. Don't worry if the stocks keep falling, he said. Just ignore it. Sooner or later they will turn around and you will make your money. Repeat this process throughout your life, Mr. Schwed wrote, and you'll end up rich.

Using Options for Financial Insurance

I've already explained why investing in your employer is a risky move. But you may not have any choice. You may receive stock or options as part of your compensation, and you may not be able to sell them for a long time. These lock-in periods can last several years.

That leaves your wealth vulnerable. Many ordinary people in this position have been nearly wiped out as a result. Their company or their industry hit a crisis and the stock collapsed.

You may want to explore ways to use financial derivatives to help protect yourself, where possible.

Very few people know how to do to this, or even think of it. It's their loss. It could have saved a lot of people who instead were wiped out in the crisis of 2008.

Financial products known as put options, which can be bought through any broker, can provide insurance against the collapse of a single company stock or an entire sector. They're like a lottery ticket that pays out only if a share price or a sector index collapses within a certain time period.

The simplest way to help insure yourself would be to buy put options in your employer's stock. You may or may not be permitted to do this by your contract. However, if you can't there is a rough workaround. You may be able to buy put options on your sector. This is easiest if there is an index or an exchange-traded fund that tracks your industry on the stock market.

The calculations can be complex. Ask your broker for help.

Does this sound like too much trouble? Staff in technology companies who bought "put" options on the NASDAQ back in 1999 and 2000 were able to keep some of their tech bubble fortunes even after the bubble burst. Any staff in the finance industry who did this before the 2008 crash may be looking at early retirement instead of looking for work.

Buying put options on your industry is far from a perfect solution. It will protect you only if the whole sector collapses. If your company gets into trouble on its own, while the rest of the industry stays aloft, it will not help.

Getting the timing right can be tricky, too. And the insurance is not free. Options cost money. Buying enough coverage to protect you until your lock-in period expires may cost quite a bit. It's worth getting expert help.

Conclusion

There are investments that can give you good long-term returns with some security and peace of mind.

Inflation-protected government bonds offer stability and guaranteed returns with no risk. They should be held where possible in a tax shelter. Where possible, buy them with a real, after-inflation yield of 2.5 percent or better.

Shares can still be a great investment, but the smartest way to invest on rising markets is through global index funds. These will give you exposure to all the world's equity markets at a low cost. That provides you the widest possible diversification. It is crazy to invest too much in the U.S. market. You already have plenty of exposure to the U.S. economy.

And there are plenty of smart, flexible funds out there where managers have genuine flexibility to move money across stocks, bonds, and other investments to find the greatest returns and avoid the biggest risks.

Covered call funds can add stabilizers to your portfolio without slowing you down. They use a strategy of buying shares and then generating income by selling derivatives against those shares. Studies have found that over recent decades this strategy has produced very good returns with lower volatility than the stock market.

Those who want to add exposure to precious metals to their portfolio may find that a managed fund that can invest in mining stocks as well as the metals gives them good returns with less risk. Metal prices alone can be volatile, while opportunities can arise in different places at different times.

More and more investors have been turning to bonds since the financial crisis broke. They are taking on a lot more complexity than you are likely to find in shares. General bond funds that manage those risks, or sector funds that focus on a particular type of bond, are two ways to maneuver the waters. Municipal bonds make a lot of sense for higher-income taxpayers, as their coupons are tax exempt.

Closed-end funds can offer some great bargains for private investors. These are mutual funds that trade on the stock market. They can often be bought for 90 cents on the dollar or even less. If you buy funds that pay out big dividends, and you reinvest those dividends, you can get very good long-term returns.

If you're worried about timing your investments, the safest way to ease your way back into the market is through regular saving each month. This is known as dollar-cost averaging.

It is worth remembering that a crisis is usually a good time to invest more money. Every financial panic feels like the end of the world. It hasn't ended yet.

Finally, those who are locked in to heavy amounts of company stock or options might want to explore whether, and how, they can use derivatives to help hedge their exposure.

CHAPTER

Cash Flow Positive from Right Now

When it comes to finances, there are two kinds of families: those burning cash, and those earning it.

Too many people are cash flow negative. They spend more than they make. Financially, they are going backwards. This describes a lot of the country. During the boom they lived off home equity withdrawals. Now that that's over they don't know what to do. These are the ones waiting for Santa Claus.

No financial advice is going to help you if you are cash flow negative. It is amazing the number of people who still fantasize that some money magic will transform their situation. This book touches on many aspects of managing your money, from protecting your assets to building a better investment portfolio, but the heart of it is right here. If you can stop burning cash and start earning it, then you will be able to secure your financial future. If you don't, you won't.

This is about turning cash flow positive. Not next month or next year. Not even tomorrow. Right now.

The key to this is taking on the three big costs burning a hole in your budget. When it comes to spending, most people are focused only on *cash* costs: the price on the sticker. But this is only one of your costs, and it is the least important. In this section we'll look at two others: opportunity cost and repeat cost. They are quiet, or hidden, costs. We'll look at the remarkable toll these take over the course of a typical lifetime.

Then we'll look at one of the most powerful things anyone can do to improve their cash flow: understanding the true value of their time.

Finally, we'll apply these ideas to a typical budget to show how anyone can cut spending, save money, and build a stronger financial future with little sacrifice. Most family budgets are stuffed full of hidden costs.

Your Hidden Costs

Personal spending has jumped by nearly 50 percent in a generation. But the item that's costing you the most money doesn't appear in your budget. It's not children, your home, or your car. It's not the Jacuzzi or the jewelry. It's not the vacation of a lifetime in Tahiti.

It's the interest you would have made on all that money if you hadn't spent it.

This point is neither glib nor an exaggeration.

A single dollar, invested at 4.5 percent above inflation, will double in about 16 years and treble in 25. Over the course of about 35 years it will grow into $5 and over 52 years it will grow to $10.

That means an 18-year-old who chooses to save $1 rather than, say, spending it on a pack of gum can expect to have about $10 more by the time he reaches 70.

Economists call this "opportunity cost," because when you spend the money you are missing out on the opportunity to invest it productively.

If we don't spend the money, it earns interest. And then the interest starts earning interest, too. And on it goes.

This opportunity or invisible cost is huge. It dwarfs the actual cash costs we pay for things. We're actually paying two, three, five, or even ten times as much.

That new Ford Mustang? The sticker cost is $21,000. But the opportunity cost is far greater. Over the next 25 years that money would have earned another $42,000. Total cost over that time: $63,000. Over 50 years it probably would have earned nine times the sticker price, taking the total cost of the Mustang to $210,000. That's some car.

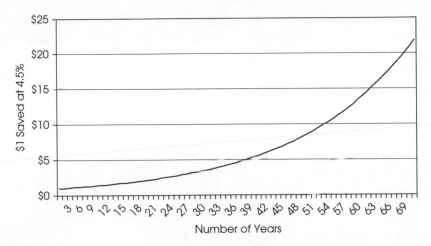

Figure 6.1   Opportunity Cost: The Lifetime Value of a Dollar

Figure 6.1 shows this in graphic form: how much a single dollar is really worth over time. Over 70 years, incredibly, $1 grows to about $22. In today's money.

And remember these calculations are in real terms, after accounting for inflation. If we used nominal figures, the results are almost poetic. If you invest $21,000 for 35 years at, say, 8 percent, you'd have $310,000. One dollar alone would become $15.

Everyone's numbers are different. It depends on your perspective, age, and circumstances. But anyone in middle age or younger needs to think in terms of many decades. As a simple rule of thumb, over about 30 years a dollar will grow to about $4 in real, inflation-adjusted terms. So if you need help keeping this principle in mind when you shop, try multiplying the price of everything you see by four.

This is a marvelously effective antidote to impulse purchases.

That $50 dinner? It's really taking $200 out of your retirement savings. That $2,000 vacation: more like $8,000. That glass ornament in the trinket shop already looked overpriced at $69.95. At $280? Are they kidding?

Many people find this simple point impossible to digest. They'll fight it bitterly. A few years back, when the iPhone first came out, I pointed out that Apple's youthful customers were taking many thousands of dollars out of their future retirement savings to buy the new product on a two-year contract. You should have heard the howls of outrage. People sent me hate mail. Bloggers—Apple fanatics, admittedly—were still raging about it two years later. People just do not want to accept the facts.

It's so much easier to think only about today and forget about tomorrow.

The good news, of course, is that this process can work in reverse. Every dollar you save now will put two, three, five, or even ten dollars back into your future pot of gold. That's the first key to rebuilding your wealth.

Repeat Costs

There is a second cost sneaking around that doesn't get a lot of attention, either: repeat cost.

Our lives are riddled with small, repeat costs that quietly take our money. It's a dollar here and a dollar there. Sometimes it seems too small to notice. Otherwise we fool ourselves by focusing on just the sticker cost instead.

Everyone knows about the $4 latte a day these days. Even if you have one only on weekdays, that will add up to about $1,000 a year.

But the psychology of repeat costs is lethal. You're never asked for that $1,000. Instead it's always just $4 today . . . and today . . . and today.

Ask someone how much they're paying for their cell phone contract and they will probably give you the wrong number. "Oh, $60," they'll say. Or: "We're paying $100, but that includes unlimited texting."

The person paying $60, of course, is really paying $60 *a month*. That's $720 a year. Someone paying $100 a month, of course, is forking out $1,200 a year.

Companies are desperate to sign up customers like you to regular contracts. They'll actually spend hefty amounts to hook you. These are called "customer acquisition costs," as if you are an item to be purchased. They know that in most cases, once you sign up, you'll stick around. And that money will quietly drain out of your account every month.

This is where the really big money is. It doesn't come from selling a small number of items with big sticker prices. It comes from lots of very small repeat costs.

Gillette, famously, doesn't make its biggest profits on the razors it sells. It makes it on the replacement blades. The oil companies who sell you a few gallons of gas at a time are worth far more than the car companies who sell you an expensive, big-ticket item only occasionally.

Cable TV companies make bigger profits than the manufacturers who produce expensive flat-screen TVs. Cellular network operators rake in bigger profits than the manufacturers of the handsets. The big money is in the small, repeat costs.

The average consumer is on the other side of this. The wealth building at your cable company comes from you.

Monthly contracts. Small daily expenses. Everybody knows in theory that these mount up quickly. But it's important to know it in practice. Television sets are cheaper than they were a generation ago. What's changed is that now we pay for cable. Many people pay $100 a month—which means $1,200 a year and $12,000 every decade.

Human nature being what it is, we have a deep-seated tendency to miss these costs or underestimate them. It's astonishing the number of people who will resist spending $50 (a cash cost) on a bread maker, and will instead spend an extra $6 a week buying each loaf from the store. The bread maker would pay for itself, and start turning a profit, by the third month.

Every year, around New Year's, financial commentators offer market thoughts and predictions for the 12 months ahead. Some even offer investment picks.

At the start of 2009 I wrote a slightly tongue-in-cheek column for the *Wall Street Journal* suggesting the best investment for the year ahead would be a Thermos.

Tongue-in-cheek, but not wrong.

They cost about $15. But if you use one to take soup to work instead of buying a sandwich, it could save you hundreds of dollars a year. The return on investment leaves any financial product in the dust.

Sometimes these costs aren't so small, either. We still underestimate them. Contrary to popular wisdom, many first-time buyers in the real estate bubble were actually able to afford their mortgages (just). What broke their budgets were all the other repeat costs of home ownership on top of the monthly mortgage payments—taxes, maintenance, condo fees, insurance. A lot of first-time buyers just overlooked them. Each one seemed manageable. In aggregate, of course, they were lethal.

Many car owners struggle to accept the full annual costs of owning and running a vehicle. It's at least $3,000, and for most people much higher. I don't even own a car, yet I constantly find myself patiently explaining to disbelieving motorists how much they are paying for insurance, taxes, maintenance, gasoline, and other expenses. They can't really get their heads around it.

Repeat costs, big or small, are so dangerous because they sneak under the radar. They are just so easy to overlook.

It doesn't stop there. That's because every repeat cost has an invisible, or opportunity, cost as well.

A few pages back I showed how a single dollar saved at 4.5 percent interest it will grow into $2, $5, or more over long periods of time. When you apply that magic to these repeat costs all around us, the numbers are explosive.

Cut $1 a month from your budget and save it instead at 4.5 percent, and after five years you'll have $66.

Over 10 years you'll have about $150. That's from just $1 a month. Over 25 years, your $1 a month will have grown to about $500. That is in today's dollars, after accounting for inflation.

Over about 35 years: $1,000.

Yes, over about 35 years just $1 a month will grow into $1,000. Instead of the rule of four discussed earlier, call this the rule of 1,000. You can see this in Figure 6.2.

What this means is pretty clear.

That cell phone bill that you think is costing you only $100 (a month) will actually end up costing you $100,000 over the course of several decades. The $200 monthly fees on your ski chalet: $200,000. The $450 monthly lease cost on your new SUV: $450,000.

It puts a new perspective on those monthly bills, doesn't it?

But every time we recapture a dollar that we were about to spend, and save it instead, we add about $4 to our future savings. Every time we capture a dollar a month of repeat cost, we add about $1,000.

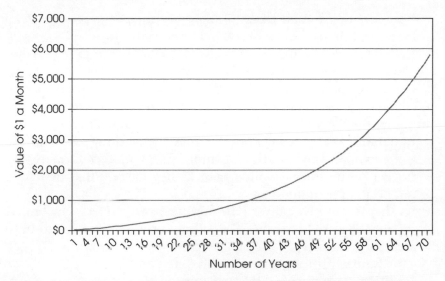

Figure 6.2   Opportunity Cost: The Lifetime Value of a Dollar a Month

And for many people it goes further still. That's because right now they're not making the maximum contribution each year to their 401(k) or equivalent savings plan at work.

If you are in this position, consider the math. If you cut a dollar a month from your expenses and contribute it to your plan, you effectively get back the income taxes you would have paid on that dollar. So the dollar a month is actually worth $1.25 a month, and over many decades maybe $1,250.

Give Yourself a Raise

Here is a simple technique to improve your financial position. Give yourself a raise, every chance you get.

How? By understanding the real value of your time—and making sure you get the best possible rate for every hour and minute.

Consider an example. More than a year into the financial crisis, the sandwich shops and cafes in many cities were still packed, every lunch hour. Clearly many people still want to buy their lunch each day. Some may feel they are simply too busy to make their own at home.

But have they done the math?

It costs maybe $8 to buy lunch in a sandwich shop.

How much do the ingredients cost to make it at home? Two dollars? So the savings are around $6.

On a daily basis, it's pretty hard to get worked up about six dollars. That's why so many shrug their shoulders each the morning and figure they'll get lunch at work. It's a classic repeat cost.

But think of this from another angle. How long does it take someone to make lunch in the morning? Ten minutes? (That would be moving pretty slowly—which may, if they haven't had their coffee yet, be a fair assumption.)

So they could save $6 with 10 minutes' work. That's an hourly rate of $36. Over six days, they'll do about an hour's work and have an extra $36.

That is nearly twice the average national wage.

And these are after-tax dollars. One of the great things about money you save, unlike money you earn, is that you don't have to pay any taxes on it. You might have to earn, say, $45 or so an hour in a traditional, taxed job to take home $36.

And this was assuming you were moving at a glacial pace through your kitchen. If it takes only five minutes to make lunch at home, then the hourly rate rockets to $72 an hour—or $96 before tax. (See Figure 6.3.)

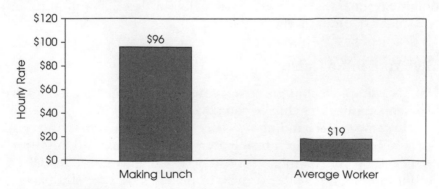

Figure 6.3   Hourly Rates: Making Lunch versus Average Worker
Data source: U.S. Department of Labor.

To put that in context, someone earning $96 an hour full-time would earn nearly $200,000 a year. I don't know how many people lining up in the sandwich shops actually make this much, but it's not many.

Yes, this matters. As we've seen, these repeat costs are enormous over time. And when you add in the opportunity costs, the results are remarkable. Six dollars a day is $30 a week and $120 a month. So over the decades it can add $120,000 to your retirement savings.

Hardly anyone clips coupons anymore. (And you can see why. The idea makes a lot of people think of eccentric elderly ladies buying cat food.) The savings are repeat costs, so they seem so small at the time. Do you really want to bother to save 50 cents on a can of soup, or $2 on some laundry detergent? Who has time?

But it's actually a high-wage activity. You're getting paid well.

How long does it take? Ten minutes a week? While sitting on the sofa, watching TV?

If it takes 10 minutes and saves you $10 off your groceries, that's an hourly rate of $60. And it's tax free. Before tax you'd have to earn maybe $75 or more in a regular job.

Who turns down the chance to get paid $75 an hour for sitting on their sofa watching TV?

This isn't fanciful. It can save you hundreds of dollars a year.

There are opportunities all around. Sometimes they aren't so obvious. But once you start valuing your time and thinking about them, they start to appear.

Do you really spend $150 to get your hair colored at the salon? If it takes two hours to do it yourself and costs you $10 instead, that's the equivalent of earning $70 an hour. Tax free. You'd have to earn a rate of more than $90 in a taxable job to get the same amount.

Or think of those loyalty programs they offer in the stores, or those new credit cards with a sign-up bonus.

They always seem like such a hassle. There are the forms to fill out, membership numbers to remember, and junk mail to throw out in due course.

But running the numbers may change your perspective.

If you drive a car, your nearest gas station may offer a credit card that will save you 5 percent on purchases. If you spend $50 a week at the gas station, that's $2.50 a week, or $10 a month. That's maybe $10,000 over many decades.

How long will it take you to sign up for the card? Even if it takes half an hour—a long time—that will save you $120 in the first year. Call that an hourly rate of $120, tax free.

(Obviously it's always worth checking the fine print. Some cards will try to sock you with an annual fee. Note that opening too many cards and closing them quickly can also hit your credit score. And it makes sense only if you are disciplined about using credit cards, and pay them off in full every month.)

One card affiliated with an airline recently offered new customers enough frequent-flier miles to fly round-trip between New York and Los Angeles. To get the miles, customers had to use their new card for $700 worth of purchases. But the ticket was worth about $600.

So long as you used the card for purchases you would make anyway, it was a terrific deal.

Let's say you spent two hours of your time signing up for the card, activating it, and making sure they credited your account with the frequent-flier miles. That's still about $300 an hour.

Tax free, of course.

Even a card that gets you 10 percent off your purchases for a month, or that earns bonus points towards a meal or a ticket, can be worth it. Most people don't do the math on their time. That's their loss.

When in doubt, work out how long something will take to do yourself and how much you'll save. Convert it to an hourly rate, and then add maybe 20 percent or 25 percent on top for taxes. If it's still not worth it, don't do it. But a lot of the time it will be.

How to Make $500,000 the Easy Way

Okay, so that's the theory. Let's take a look this in practice. We're going to make you half a million dollars with very little sacrifice.

How? By going through some of the major spending areas in a typical middle-class budget, and finding about $500 a month in savings. Forget all that talk about living on cardboard. Most of these savings come with little or no pain.

Fire Your Banker

These days, a lot of people might like to fire their banker for nothing. Would you do it for $20,000?

Changing banks can easily cut $20 a month in repeat costs. And we know what that's really costing you over the course of your life.

Willie Sutton famously said he robbed banks "because that's where the money is."

He was right, of course. And guess where it came from.

Account maintenance fees. Miscellaneous charges. Zero, or minuscule, interest. These are the kinds of small-change issues that most people ignore because they seem so petty. You're busy. You don't have time to go chasing after every item.

But that, of course, is what the banks rely on. Bankrate.com says the average service fee is $12 a month. Many families maintain several accounts, one in each name.

ATM fees: If you use the machine of another bank, you can end up paying two sets of fees: one to your bank, and another to the bank whose ATM you just used.

This is for access to *your own* money. Twice a month at maybe $3 a time.

Then take a look at the interest you're earning (or not) on your checking account.

The average interest rate on a checking account that earns any interest at all is an absurd 0.16 percent, according to a study by Bankrate.com.

Bounced check fee? Twenty-nine bucks.

"This is low-hanging fruit when it comes to squeezing every penny out of your budget," Greg McBride, senior analyst at Bankrate, told me. "In terms of carelessness, people can easily see hundreds of dollars a year drained out of their account through carelessness. ATM fees, bounced check charges, monthly service fees—it's all avoidable."

No wonder business consultant Gary Hamel could tell a conference of bankers in 2006 that their "biggest profit center" was "customer ignorance."[*]

---

[*]Gary Hamel, BAI Retail Delivery Conference, November 2006.

So-called free checking isn't quite as bad. You pass up (minuscule) interest but save on rip-off fees. Yet it's often still a poor deal. Free checking just means the bank gets free use of your money.

It's sitting idle. That's costing you money.

Most people keep their money in a traditional bank simply because that's the way they've always done it. The banks love that inertia. It helps them pad their profits. Dissatisfied? Shop around.

Check out local credit unions and cooperative savings banks, low-cost online banks such as ING Direct, and even money market accounts operated by brokerage firms. These may offer much better rates of interest and lower fees.

I'll confess I have so little trust in the big for-profit banks these days that I now gravitate toward local institutions that don't operate for profit. That includes credit unions, mutual savings banks, and savings and loans. I figure I won't have to watch them like a hawk every moment. It's uncanny the way every major bank with a $20-million-a-year CEO to support seems to sneak extra fees into your account when you're not looking.

You don't have to go to a big bank to get access to an ATM network. Most online banks have agreements that give you access to ATMs in your neighborhood. And so do many credit unions and mutual savings banks.

Take a look at your local credit unions. They may give you a better banking deal. Credit unions have no shareholders (they are owned by their customers), so they pay no dividends or corporate income taxes. They can pass on savings to their customers.

They also save a lot of the money that the big banks waste on marketing. Credit unions exist by state or federal charter, and they are generally restricted to taking customers from certain defined groups—such as people with a connection to a particular town, company, or industry.

Credit unions also enjoy federal deposit insurance, as banks do. You can find out more details from the Credit Union National Association at www.cuna.org.

Squeeze Your Insurance

You are probably paying too much for your home and auto insurance. Most people are.

Insurance really adds up. The average car insurance policy costs $820 per vehicle, according to the Insurance Information Institute, the industry organization. Homeowners' insurance? About $760 a year.

This is dead money. Just 5 percent or so of homeowners make a claim under homeowners' insurance each year. Meanwhile those premium dollars are padded with waste. Out of every dollar consumers spend on car insurance, just 64 cents go to pay claims. The rest goes for insurance company expenses, taxes, and profits.

The figures for homeowners' insurance are even worse. Just 53 cents per dollar go on claims. Expenses take another 29 cents. The rest is taxes and profits.

There are three simple techniques to save money.

First: Shop around. It's the old line, but it's still true. Insurance policy rates vary enormously from company to company. You may find you can slash the amount you are spending without any loss of coverage at all. Make sure you are comparing like with like, and factor in any differences in coverage.

Many people, maybe most, could cut their insurance rates by moving carriers.

The second technique? Raise your deductibles. For most consumers, this is a quick win.

"Raising your deductibles is a really smart way to save money on insurance," Jean Salvatore of the Insurance Information Institute told me. "It's an immediate way of reducing what you pay."

The rewards are out of all proportion to the risks. In some cases, raising the deductibles by a few hundred dollars a year will actually cut the premiums by nearly the same amount.

The Institute estimates that if you raise the deductible on your car insurance from $200 to $500, you can probably cut your premiums on collision and comprehensive coverage by about 15 percent to 30 percent. If you raise your deductible to $1,000, you can save 40 percent. This can mean hundreds of dollars saved per year.

And the math is pretty similar for home insurance, too. You're getting a poor deal if you have a deductible of less than $500. If you raise it from $500 to $1,000, according to Insurance Information Institute data, you'll often cut your premiums by about 25 percent. Most people set their deductibles way too low to be efficient. They're suffering from money illusion. They're worrying about the risk of small losses. But they're missing the major savings.

If you spend $2,000 a year on insurance, cutting that by 15 percent is $300 a year. That's $25 a month. It doesn't sound like much—until you think about what it builds into over time.

It's in the interest of the insurance companies to cut you a good deal if you raise your deductibles. Small claims account for a big share of insurance waste. They cost a lot in staff time, and staples, to process. And they are harder to check for fraud. Those carrying high deductibles are signaling that they aren't going to waste the insurance company's time and costs on a lot of petty claims.

It works for customers, too. While most customers make a claim rarely, when they do it tends to be big. On homeowners' insurance, the average, in 2005, stemmed from storm damage and came to about $6,900.

The smart way to use insurance is to spend less on premiums, and keep coverage to the big-ticket items.

The third way to squeeze money on insurance: Call up your insurance company and pressure them for a discount.

It may be that simple. You may already qualify. For example, if you have gone several years without filing a claim, or you're retired, they may give you money off. Your homeowners insurer may also give you a discount if you've installed dead-bolt locks or burglar alarms, or you have moved jewelry to a safe-deposit box. They may cut you a deal if you offer to give them your car insurance business, too.

They may just cut you a deal if you threaten to leave. You won't know till you've tried.

If you can save $400 a year, that's nearly $33 a month.

Shop Online

Looking for more savings? Try moving your shopping online. It's usually cheaper than visiting traditional, bricks-and-mortar stores. Online resellers have lower costs than traditional retailers. They don't have to pay for real estate. They don't have to pay for so much staff.

Shopping online is also easier and quicker. There's more available. It doesn't matter where you live: No mall or city offers anything like the same range.

You don't have to get in a car, fight traffic, or park. You don't have to pay for cappuccinos when you shop from your living room.

You don't have to hunt fruitlessly for an available and sanitary bathroom.

And you're less likely to make impulse purchases. You're not holding the item in your hand, after all. You're not being bombarded with the music, and sales patter, and other inducements of the retail experience. And of course there's no instant gratification. An online purchase isn't a trophy. You won't see it for several days, anyway.

Yes, shopping online is a bit dull. That's the point.

It's far easier to compare prices online. You don't have to run from store to store to check which one is cheapest. It just takes the click of a mouse. And this is where the really incredible deals are. You can save by using coupon and shopping deal web sites. They include:

- Coupons.com (http://print.coupons.com)
- CouponSurfer (http://couponsurfer.com)
- PPGazette.com (www.ppgazette.com)
- CouponCabin (www.couponcabin.com)
- DealzConnection.com (www.dealzconnection.com)
- Valpak (www.valpak.com)
- DealCatcher.com (www.dealcatcher.com)
- Currentcodes.com (www.currentcodes.com)
- CouponMom.com (www.couponmom.com)
- SmartSource.com (coupons2.smartsource.com)
- Groupon.com (www.groupon.com)
- Buywithme.com (www.buywithme.com

New sites are being launched all the time. They reward the savvy shopper. Start first with Retailmenot.com, whose data comes from ordinary customers. They send in coupon codes and online deal scoops. This makes it a pretty good search engine for coupons.

If you shop online, you can typically save between 1 and 3 percent by using a rebates web site such as eBates or Fatwallet. These collect the click-through referral fees from shopping web sites and then share them with you, the customer. If you spend $3,000 online in a year, that can easily be worth $100. Membership is free. Online retailers also offer cards that give back 3 percent of what you spend at their site.

It's not much. But even if it saves you only $20 a month, that's another $20,000 over time.

Rethink Cable

If you can bear to go without cable TV altogether, you could accumulate another $100,000 in lifetime savings pretty easily.

This is a classic repeat cost. We barely notice it. But the cumulative effect, as we've seen, is enormous.

The alternative isn't to sit in the dark.

More and more TV programs and movies are available for free on the Internet. Web sites like Hulu.com, Sling.com, and Veoh.com are turning into online broadcasters. The TV companies themselves are starting to put more and more of their programs on their web sites. (They have to, to compete with all the pirate stations from Asia.) With some simple cables you can connect a computer to your TV and still watch them on the bigger screen.

On a monthly basis it might not seem worth it. But when you consider the full value of the repeat costs it might.

Set-top boxes that can access the Internet can also replace your monthly cable bill. Apple TV is one example. It can download podcasts, movies, and TV programs. Others are being launched all the time. If you spend $200 on the box and it saves you $60 or $100 a month, the payback is pretty quick and the return on your investment is impressive.

Podcasts, obviously, are free. There's a growing number of video podcasts. It costs money to rent or buy movies from iTunes, but you could get quite a lot of programming for the amount you'll save on cable. And it isn't a subscription. You aren't quietly bleeding money. You pay only for what you use. And when you have to pay for each program you watch, you end up being more judicious.

When the financial crisis hit, Internet movie rental service Netflix started booming, too. It's much cheaper than cable, often costing $20 or less per month. This alone can save hundreds of dollars a year. Netflix has a huge library of TV programs as well as movies. Quite a lot can be watched online for no extra charge as part of your subscription.

Network TV is still free, as always. In most places this means a good range of channels from CBS to PBS. Network TV shows more than many realize, but it's less convenient than cable because the programs aren't always on when you want to watch them. Cheap technology helps here, too. A simple $90 DVD recorder and a stack of DVDs solves that problem.

Many people get cable for the sports. They'll have to weigh the cost against the benefit. And in order to get the sports package, they typically have to sign up for the basic programming as well. Following the team may be costing $700 to $1,000 a year.

It's always worth doing the math. How many games do you actually watch? If it's, say, 50 a year, you may be paying as much as $20 a game.

The sports franchises are as eager to free themselves from the domination of the cable companies as you are. Broadband Internet makes that possible. Most of the big leagues will sell you a package that lets you watch games live online. Usually these cost somewhere between $80 and $120 for the season. Some also let you sign up for a game or a week. Visit the likes of NHL.com, NBA.com, MLB.com, and NFL.com to see what's on offer.

The costs are still pretty high. But the leagues have to compete with online pirate sites that stream games illegally for free. That keeps a lid on how much they can charge. It may be more cost-effective to pay for an online pass than for cable every month.

And there's always radio. It's how past generations followed baseball.

Okay, everybody's budget is different. Let's score this one $50 a month.

Cut Your Phone Bills

Long distance phone calls used to be so expensive that middle-class families made them sparingly and hurried them up.

These days you can sit in your living room and make a video call to Australia for free.

Yet the average American family now spends three times more on phone bills than they did 25 years ago—about $1,100 a year. Crazy.

These are repeat costs ripe for savings.

A surprising number of people still have traditional landlines, even though they also have Internet access at home. This is pure waste. You can use the Internet to make free, or nearly free, phone calls using Voice over Internet Protocol (VoIP). There are a growing number of services that offer calls for little or nothing. The best known include Skype and GoogleTalk. All you will need is a special phone. These can be as cheap as $20. Some plug into your computer, while others operate as stand-alone devices that access your Internet connections directly.

Savings: maybe $40 a month.

Cellular phones are not as easy to replace. But you have to look at how much it's costing you, and whether it is worth it. This is a classic repeat cost. The money leaks out of your account every month. We have become used to the expense, as if it is unavoidable.

Many people who have a cell phone or BlackBerry through work still pay extra for their own phone as well. Why? A prepaid phone instead of a contract could save you serious cash. Some providers will offer 1,000 minutes you can use anytime for $100. It will keep you in touch without costing too much.

Savings: maybe $80 a month.

Many mobile phones can access wireless Internet networks, too. You can use them to make free, or nearly free, Voice over Internet calls at nearby WiFi hotspots.

If you have a mobile phone contract, here are two other tricks.

Call your provider and tell them you want to leave. They will almost certainly put you through to a customer service person whose job is to keep you. He or she should try to cut you a deal. Remember, you are a very profitable customer for the cell phone operator no matter how little you spend. That's because they have already spent billions building their networks. Now they need all the revenue they can get.

Even if they just give you a $50 credit, that's worth an extra $200 in your retirement account. And getting it is a good use of your time. Do the math. If it takes you 15 minutes on the phone—10 of them on hold, of course—that's an hourly rate of $200 an hour. Tax free.

The second technique: If you are due for a free phone upgrade, get the one with the biggest subsidy and just sell it on eBay. Then carry on using your old phone. It's a free $100.

Overall, let's average this one at $40 a month. Some people can save a lot more.

Leave the Plastic at Home

We all fritter money away. Impulse purchases. Nickel-and-dime stuff. And it adds up.

Many financial advisers urge their clients to keep a diary of everything they spend for a month. It's pretty good advice—for some people. (The results are usually an eye-opener. Typical response: "We spent how much eating out?")

But a lot of people won't do it. They'll say, "That's a great idea," then forget about it. Or they'll do it for two days and then give up. They'll lose the notebook, maybe accidentally on purpose.

Very few people have the temperament needed to keep an accurate diary. Those who do are rarely the ones with the budget problems.

We're looking for easier, oven-ready solutions. Here's one.

Just leave the plastic at home. The credit cards. The debit cards. Even the ATM card. Carry only cash.

If you want to make sure you spend only, say, $100 a week on incidentals, then go to the bank on Wednesday, take out $100, and live on that. Do not carry any cards outside the home.

(The reason for taking money out on Wednesday, incidentally, is that it means you will still have enough left to enjoy the weekend, and if you blow your remaining cash on the weekend you won't have to last too much longer until you can get more.)

It puts a new spin on the old American Express advertising slogan, "Don't leave home without it." These days maybe your slogan should be "Don't leave home with it." If you can't do that, exactly how were you planning to stick to a budget? If you are really worried about emergencies, you can always try folding a single check into a pocket for true desperation.

Not having plastic with you will pretty effectively clamp down on impulse purchases.

And, of course, it will make it much harder to spend money on credit, because you won't have your credit card with you.

The number of payments with credit and debit cards doubled just between 2000 and 2006.* It was no coincidence at all that this

---

*Federal Reserve Payments Studies, 2005, 2007.

was when consumer spending exploded. Go back a generation or two and it was very different. In 1970 just one family in six had a credit card. And they used them rarely.

Sure, cards can be valuable for making certain remote transactions. If you want to buy something over the Internet, or by phone, it's a little hard to use cash or a check. But so what? You don't have to cut up all your cards. You can just leave them at home.

(If you cannot handle credit cards at all, and keep carrying a balance from month to month, the situation is different. In that circumstance you should just cut them up completely. Have only a debit card—and leave that at home.)

If you're blowing $50 a week and you don't know where it's going, that's about $200 a month. Saving 10 percent is another $20 in monthly repeat costs. Over time that's worth a lot of money.

Declare a Holiday Truce

Legend has it that on Christmas Day, 1914, soon after the start of the First World War in Europe, troops on both sides declared an unofficial truce. For a few hours, they stopped shooting at each other. In places along the western front, they actually wandered out into no-man's-land to exchange greetings and drinks. Some, it's said, even kicked a soccer ball around.

It was the last Christmas truce in history. Today, instead, the holiday season has been weaponized. Heaven help the person who launches the lesser gift on December 25.

Can you get friends and family to agree to a Christmas truce? It will put a lot of extra money in your pocket each year.

It may be one thing to buy presents for children, especially young children. But why are you buying anything for Aunt Sally? Or your brother-in-law? And why are they buying anything for you?

What should be a festive and relaxed time of the year is turned into a misery as you battle into the busiest shopping malls and precincts to find gifts for near and distant family members. "Have you got anything for Aunt Sue? Will Cousin Bob expect something? What are we getting for the baby?"

This is money wasted. It's some of the purest waste in your entire year's budget.

According to the National Retail Federation, the average American spends about $800 each Christmas. Most of that, about $630, goes for presents.

Christmas is the only thing keeping a lot of stores in business. The Friday after Thanksgiving, the first day of the Christmas shopping season, is known among retailers as Black Friday. That's because it is, more or less, the day when retailers finally move into the black, or profit, for the year.

From January 1 through the last Thursday of November, they barely make enough money to cover their costs. Not until the silver bells start ringing—and ringing, and ringing—do they actually move into profits.

The amount spent on Christmas presents may be shocking, but the real offense is the amount wasted.

Ties that will never be worn. Sweaters with reindeers on them. "Italian Stallion" golf balls. Ghastly embroidered cushions. If you don't believe me, look around your local mall next December. The sheer crap piled high on every shelf can hardly be believed. It's hard to accept that anyone buys this stuff—but they obviously do, or the retailers wouldn't order more each year.

"It's only a bit of money," people say as they fork out $10, $20, or $100 for items that no one will want.

A fascinating study by Yale economics professor Joel Waldfogel in the early 1990s discovered something both hilarious and alarming. He put a figure on the waste. It's between 10 percent and 30 percent of the amount spent on presents.[*]

The logic? He looked at how much was spent on presents, and how little the recipients would have been willing to spend for the same items. The gap, in economists' terms, is called "deadweight loss." If you've spent $100 buying me something for which I would have paid only $70, you've thrown away $30.

A deadweight loss of 30 percent on the annual Christmas haul of $630 per person comes to $190. (That's $16 a month, or $16,000 in lifetime savings.)

---

[*]Joel Waldfogel, "The Deadweight Loss of Christmas," *American Economic Review* (December 1993).

The giving of gifts on December 25 is a retailer's racket. We're being conned into thinking that somehow it is traditional. In fact, it's pretty new, what's called an invented tradition.

Most of it got commercialized in the 1920s. Jesus wasn't even born on December 25. Various theories say March or September. Christmas Day just coincides, sort of, with the pagan holiday of Saturnalia.

If you can't get a Christmas truce, you may still be able to save by giving gifts that get the biggest bang for your buck.

Give your labor. Help a technologically challenged relative set up a Skype account. Offer to mow Grandma's lawn, or to look after your sister's children for a day, or to paint your mom's living room.

Giving your labor makes a great gift, and it costs you absolutely no money. It's really hard to find someone reliable, trustworthy, and competent to come into your home to paint your living room or look after your children. The offer is actually incredibly valuable.

It's also personal. Giving your labor involves a lot less of your money, but a lot more of you.

Your Aunt Sally would have to earn maybe $50 in order to pay someone $35 to mow her lawn. But if you perform the labor directly, there's no tax to pay.

If you have a craft or skill, make presents. But think twice before giving your art. People may not want to hang your particular item on their wall. And there is no easy way for them to say so. Think three times before making an item of clothing for someone (unless you dislike them intensely, of course).

Give other cashless presents—like spare frequent-flier miles.

Or at least give gift vouchers. It is a sign of how crazy the holidays have become that these are looked down on as presents. They are actually among the few that make any sense.

You wouldn't order for someone else at a restaurant. Yet, come December, you presume to know what they'd like.

Vouchers don't entail any deadweight loss. That's because the money is spent by the recipient. And they come with another benefit. They are probably worth more than any other gift, because they can be spent after Christmas—in the sales.

One of the most surreal aspects of the holiday season is the way in which we knowingly, even willingly, choose to overpay for products for no legitimate reason. Every time we buy a present for Christmas

Day instead of waiting until January, we waste maybe 10 percent of the cost. That's at least as far as prices fall the moment the holiday rush is over. If you're spending $600 a year, that's $60. That's free money.

Whenever I take on the Christmas madness, someone accuses me of being a Grinch. How ironic. Everyone has heard of the Dr. Seuss story *How the Grinch Stole Christmas*.

The Grinch was the one who thought that Christmas was all about the presents.

Dining In Is the New Going Out

If you're a typical household, you could save at least $50 a month just by skipping one restaurant meal. And that's just an inexpensive meal for two at a midmarket place. Fill in your own numbers.

Restaurants are as bad for the wallet as they are for the waistline.

This one change may be all you need to right your finances.

Dining out is terrible economics. Consider how much you are paying and what you get.

A look through the accounts of big restaurant companies like Darden, which owns Olive Garden and Red Lobster, tells the tale. Just a third of what the customers spend goes on the food and drink. A third. The rest goes on rent, labor, miscellaneous costs, and profit.

That's not counting the tip, either.

These figures are pretty typical for the industry.

In recent decades the middle-class American kitchen has been transformed. Many people have designer fridges and ranges, and ovens so complex it takes ten minutes to find the button for "bake." We have programmable microwaves, Italian espresso machines, and electric juicers. And of course, we live in bigger and more comfortable homes, with bigger and better dining areas. Then we go out to eat.

Call it $50.

Save on the Basics

If you can save just 10 percent on your groceries and other household basics, how much will that add to your cash flow? Forty dollars a month? More?

The savings are really easy to find.

Cut out expensive brands. You can often find a no-brand product for half the price of the name-brand product. Most consumers think the cheaper product must be lower-quality. But that's not always the case. It is often simply a better deal.

Food companies spend vast sums of money each year to con you into overpaying for something you could buy more cheaply.

Charlie Munger, the partner of super investor Warren Buffett, said a few years back that many food businesses were simply terrific to invest in. Many of the companies lived comfortable lives, didn't compete too strenuously, and raked in huge profits. General Mills, which makes cereals, frozen pizzas, and snacks, boasts fat gross margins of about 36 percent. Kraft's groceries division: 31 percent.

Oftentimes in a supermarket the no-name brand is similar to the famous brand. Sometimes it is exactly the same. They are sometimes made in the same factory.

Time and again, blind taste tests find no real difference.

Try going without the name-brand products at the supermarket for a month. Buy only generics. In one or two cases, at the end you'll go back to a preferred brand. In others, you'll wonder why you were paying so much more for the same thing. This is free money.

Clip coupons. As we've seen, this is a high-value use of your time. It's easy. And if it saves you $10 a week on your groceries that's $40 a month.

Stock up. Supermarkets put different products on sale at different times. They'll take a loss on some products to get you into the store—so they can charge you full price for everything else. Beat them at their own game: When a product goes on sale, buy it in bulk (if it will keep) and stock up. After a while you won't have to buy much at full price.

Buying in bulk at discount clubs like Sam's Club and Costco is another easy way to save money. It is much cheaper for companies to sell you 24 rolls of paper towels at a time than two or four rolls at a time.

Sign up for loyalty programs. As we've seen, these can save you good money over time.

Steal Beauty

If you get your hair colored in a professional salon, how much does it cost you? A hundred dollars? Two hundred?

As mentioned earlier, you can pay yourself a terrific hourly wage by doing this yourself.

This is a classic repeat cost. If you spend $150 a time and you get your hair colored every six weeks, that's $1,300 a year. Yes, those numbers are correct.

That's just over $100 a month. And of course it means that over many decades your hair is costing you $100,000, maybe more.

Sure, it looks nice. But $100,000 nice?

Coloring your hair at home, yourself, may seem far less glamorous. It may even *be* less glamorous. But having an extra $100,000 in your retirement account in 30 years' time may take the sting out of the misery.

Good drugstore brands for hair color, like Garnier and L'Oreal Preference, can achieve a similar result for $10. Or you can buy the professional hair colors from a specialist chain like Sally's Beauty Supply.

Oh, and getting your nails done? If you spend $15 once every two weeks, that's another $30 a month. It's costing you $30,000 over 35 years. Your nails: $30,000.

In total, call this one $50 a month. And I'm probably lowballing it.

Bread and Coffee

How much does your family spend on bread from the store? If you go through, say, three $2.50 loaves a week, that's $7.50. (If you have teenagers in the house or you buy organic ciabatta somewhere fancy, like Whole Foods, the numbers may be much higher.) That's $30 a month.

This may be the easiest repeat cost to eliminate in your entire budget.

Bread machines sell for as little as $50, and they cost cents to run. The only ingredient that's likely to cost much is the yeast. Buy it in bulk and keep it in the freezer.

If making your own bread saves you $6 a week (accounting for ingredients), that's about $24 a month.

The savings aren't huge, but they are almost free. The time and effort involved in making your own bread are minuscule. The bread is actually better than most of the stuff you buy in the store.

Or, to put it another way, if a $50 bread machine saves you $6 a week, it will save you $312 a year. After deducting the cost, that's a return of more than 500 percent on your investment. Wall Street's lucky to get 10 percent.

There's a similar approach when it comes to the infamous "latte a day" that personal finance commentators always talk about.

No, don't give up on $4 coffees. Just make your own.

You can buy a cappuccino machine these days for $150. A lot of people may not want to spend that money. But not doing so is a false economy. The sticker cost looks bigger than the repeat cost, but actually it's much smaller.

Savings: $4 a day, $20 a week, or roughly $80 a month.

You're in profit by the end of month two. After that, your cappuccino machine is making money as well as coffee.

And you're still drinking a latte a day.

Average this at $50 saved each month—including bread, and all those lattes.

Get a Free Energy Audit

Finally, you can make some free savings by asking your local power company for a free home energy audit.

They are often happy to do this. They find it easier to help you to cut your consumption than to persuade voters to approve a new power plant.

We are the energy junkies of the world. The average American uses twice as much fuel each year as an Italian, Brit, or Japanese.

Some energy economies are easy. Like air-drying your dishes. It cuts the power consumption of a dishwasher by half. Or using water-efficient shower heads. The Department of Energy's Energy Efficiency and Renewable Energy (EERE) web site (www.eere .energy.gov) offers a lot of tips. Or switching off all electronics, such as computers, cable boxes, and TVs, at the plug each night. As long as they are on standby they are drawing power and costing you money.

The average American household spends about $1,800 a year on energy. (That's not even counting fuel for vehicles.) Cut it by 10 percent and that's another $15 a month saved.

Adding It All Up

These are not heroic cost cuts. They do not involve living under a bridge and eating cold noodles. Many of the savings come with little or no sacrifice at all. And each, on its own, may seem trivial or small.

But these are repeat costs. And when you combine repeat costs with the enormous opportunity costs, the lifetime savings are huge. Take a look.

- *Making lunch.* We saved an easy $72 a month.
- *Firing your banker.* Maybe $20 a month changing banks.
- *Squeezing your insurance.* Another $33.
- *Shopping online.* Maybe $20.
- *Rethinking cable.* We scored this as $50 a month, though you could probably go higher.
- *Cutting your phone bills.* Score it $40.
- *Leaving the plastic at home.* If you can cut out $20 a month in frittered expenses, that's an easy win.
- *Having a holiday truce.* About $16 a month.
- *Dining in.* Skipping one restaurant meal a month will save at least $50.
- *Saving at the supermarket.* Ten dollars a week would save $40 a month. Score working the loyalty programs as $30, though it could go a lot higher.
- *Stealing beauty.* Easily $50 a month.
- *Bread and coffee.* Another $50 a month.
- *Energy.* A 10 percent cut is $15 a month.

Total savings: Just over $500 a month, or around $6,000 a year.

Over 20 years that may be worth $200,000, in today's money. Over 35 years, thanks to the rule of 1,000, it could grow to around half a million dollars. In retirement, that will pay you an income of $25,000 a year.

Compare that with the current situation, where most people haven't even been able to set aside $50,000.

And the gains may not end there. Anyone currently struggling under credit card debt is going to realize extra gains, because this cash flow will liberate them. They will be saving themselves 12 percent interest or more on their debt.

Many people will get an extra benefit. Right now they may not be able to make the maximum contributions to their 401(k) plans at work because they are spending that money to live. But that means they are missing out on a tax break, and maybe some employers' contributions as well. They are leaving money on the table.

If these savings liberate them to the point where they are able to max out their 401(k) contributions each year, then they will be worth even more than these numbers indicate. It's all good when you start generating cash.

Further Thoughts

How Much Is Your Car Costing You?

Cars are cash guzzlers. They are a terrible deal. Few realize just how much they really cost.

The purchase price. The cost of gas, insurance, and maintenance. Parking, and parking tickets. Registration and taxes. Tolls and new tires.

It adds up. The American Automobile Association (AAA) says the average new car owner is paying about $7,800 a year. That's assuming you finance the purchase and drive a fairly typical 15,000 miles a year. They put the figure as low as about $5,000 a year for a small sedan like a Honda Civic or a Ford Focus, and as high as $9,400 a year for a large sedan like a Nissan Maxima.

These figures include about $1,000 for insurance; $500 for license, registration, and taxes; and about 14.5 cents a mile for gas, maintenance, and tires.

Everyone's math is going to look a little different. The AAA numbers include about $3,400 a year for depreciation on a new car.

It's much more sensible to buy a used car. But the costs are still higher than most people realize.

If someone pays $10,000 for a used car and keeps it for 10 years, the true cost of the purchase isn't just $1,000 a year. When you include the opportunity cost on that money, it's actually nearer

$1,500 a year instead. A good rule of thumb is that if you keep a car for 10 years, it actually costs you about $150 a year for each $1,000 of the purchase price.

Bottom line? According to the federal government, the typical family spends about $7,600 on vehicles. That includes purchases and running costs.

What can you do?

- Remember cars are a liability. Some people will buy the best they can afford. You're better off buying the cheapest you can get away with. New cars, of course, are almost always a terrible deal: A new car typically loses thousands of dollars in value the moment you drive it off the lot. If you drive an old clunker you can save on insurance, too.
- Can you get rid of a car if you have more than one? It may not be easy to get along with fewer cars. Anyone who lives outside of a big city is probably going to need one for each adult in the home. But if you can do without one of the family cars, you're going to save maybe $3,000 or $4,000 a year.
- And if you really want to be radical, can you move to a location where you don't need a car at all? In some cities you can pretty much survive on foot. They include Chicago, Boston, New York, and Washington, D.C. Car rental, or an hourly car service like Zipcar, can provide all the wheels some people need.

  Sure, the real estate costs more. But if you don't need to spend $8,000 a year on two cars, you may come out ahead. That money will pay the interest on a $160,000 mortgage at 5 percent interest. Factor in the tax break on mortgage interest and it may even cover a $200,000 loan.

Is Your Vacation Home an Asset or a Liability?

Millions of people own a second home—in the sun, by the lake, or in the mountains. The attraction is obvious.

But if you are looking for ways to save money, you may find you are better off selling it.

Obviously, recent years have been difficult times to sell real estate in many parts of the country.

Prices have collapsed in some choice areas for vacation properties, including Florida and areas of the West. But keeping ownership is still probably costing you a lot of money. You should look at the math.

Ownership has to be financed one way or another. If you took out a mortgage, you have to pay the interest as well as the principal. If you paid cash, then that's money you can't invest elsewhere, so you are missing out on profits.

Property taxes vary a lot, but often come to around 1.5 percent of the value.

And then you have other annual costs. If you own a house, you will have to pay for insurance, maintenance, and upkeep. If you own a condo, you have to pay condo fees that factor those costs in. This is often 2 percent of the purchase price per year as well.

Net result: Your vacation home may actually cost you about 8.5 percent of the purchase price every year. Even with tax breaks on property taxes and mortgage interest, the annual costs may come to about 7.5 percent.

During the days when real estate values kept going up and up, that didn't matter so much. Most years, you made more on house price inflation than you paid in costs. You could congratulate yourself on your wisdom in buying early. You were basically being paid to own the home.

If that doesn't continue, the math will look very different.

The long-term returns on real estate have traditionally been only 2.5 percent above inflation. If that's the performance in the future, you may be paying 5 percent of the purchase price each year for the use of the home. But oftentimes you can get a much better deal renting.

Conclusion

Your only reliable source of cash flow is you. If you want to have any hope of putting your finances on a sound footing, you need to turn cash flow positive right now.

Doing that means tackling your costs head-on. Remember that two of your biggest costs are below the radar screen: Opportunity costs and repeat costs dwarf the prices you see on the stickers.

Three principles to remember:

1. *The rule of four:* When you include the opportunity cost, any dollar you spend is going to end up costing your four times as much.
2. *The rule of 1,000:* When you include the opportunity cost on the money, a repeat cost of $1 a month will end up costing you $1,000. And if you weren't maxing out your 401(k) already, it's costing you even more—maybe $1,250.
3. *Give yourself a raise:* If you understand the true value of your time, you can make sure you get the best possible rate for it.

CHAPTER 7

Cover Your Assets

What's the difference between a tax break and a loophole? Easy. A loophole is what the other guy gets. You? You're just getting a fair tax break.

People have become pretty cynical about the laws and the tax code these days. You can see why. During the 2008–2009 crisis, one of the most widespread refrains was, "Where's my bailout?" But Wall Street banks don't get *all* the help. There are still a few loopholes in there for the ordinary Joe and Joanna. They can be more valuable than many people realize.

In turbulent times, it's too easy to forget to take the breaks that are available to you. But they can actually be more useful, and important, than ever. It's worth making sure you squeeze the most out of them.

Why Tax Shelters Are More Important Than Ever

Tax shelters aren't just as important as they used to be. They're *more* important. Why? Five reasons.

First, they are sheltered from creditors as well as from taxes. And for a lot of people that, alas, is going to be important. No one wants to end up in bankruptcy, but at some points recently as many as 20,000 American families have been doing that every week. The earlier you put money into a shelter, the safer it will be. Even if you avoid bankruptcy, holding your money in shelters will strengthen your hand if you have to negotiate with lenders at any stage. (It will also help if someone sues you. In our lawsuit culture that can happen to anyone at any time.)

Second, tax shelters save you much more money when they are used to shelter bonds rather than stocks. During the boom, some financial advisers downplayed the tax advantages of shelters like individual retirement accounts (IRAs). They figured everybody was going to hold all their money in the stock market anyway.

After all, if the Dow was going to 36,000, why would anyone own bonds? And stocks already enjoyed favorable tax treatment. Dividends and capital gains are taxed at low rates. So shelters weren't as important.

These days, of course, investors know more about the risks of keeping all your money on the stock market. They are, and should be, keeping some in bonds instead. But bonds, except for municipals, don't enjoy favorable tax treatment. Instead, they get hit hard. They generate most of their return through interest payments, rather than capital gains, and interest is taxed at ordinary income rates.

Keeping bonds in a tax shelter dramatically transforms the long-term returns. Consider someone in a 25 percent federal tax bracket who invests $10,000 for 30 years in bonds paying 6 percent interest. In a taxable account the investor will end up with about $37,400. In a tax shelter: $57,400, or $20,000 more.

And, of course, you pay tax on the nominal interest, regardless of any inflation. So if a bond pays 6 percent but inflation also averages 6 percent, you won't make any money in real terms. But you will still be taxed as if you did. You will pay tax on the full 6 percent unless the bond is sheltered.

Tax shelters are most important when it comes to individual Treasury Inflation-Protected Securities (TIPS) bonds. That's because with TIPS you can get taxed even on supposed income you don't actually receive for years. The value of TIPS bonds gets adjusted twice a year to reflect any inflation. That increase in value counts as taxable income when it occurs—even though you don't see any actual money for it until you sell the bond or it matures. Where possible, you should always try to hold TIPS in a tax shelter.

The third reason tax shelters are more important than they used to be? Taxes are likely to rise—and that's probably going to affect stocks as well as bonds. These gigantic federal deficits will have to be paid for in one way or another. The higher the tax rates, the more valuable the shelters.

Fourth, money in your tax shelters like an IRA or a 401(k) doesn't count against you in the federal formula when your children are applying for financial aid for college. Parents are expected to contribute a certain percentage of their assets under the Effective Family Contribution (EFC) rules. Money in an IRA or a 401(k) is invisible. Money in a regular investment account isn't.

There's a fifth reason why shelters are more important in a tough economy than in a boom. It is so rarely mentioned that it is worth looking at in detail. Indeed many people, even those in finance, have never considered it at all.

Tax shelters are progressive. That's because income tax rates are progressive. The poorer you are in retirement, the more your tax shelters will pay you.

During the boom, a lot of people worried about what they were going to do when they became rich. The hubris was remarkable. Today they're giving a lot more thought to something much more relevant—how to avoid ending up poor.

When you move investments into a tax shelter, you make a trade. Your investment gains aren't taxed each year. But when you come to withdraw the money in retirement, it's taxed as ordinary income (the exception to this is a Roth IRA). When you read about this in the financial media, and hear about it from certain financial gurus, you will hear this criticized because such withdrawals are subject to income tax rates "up to 35 percent." It's true, but it's also deeply misleading. It's a sign of how a lot of financial advice you read has become disconnected from the lives that ordinary people lead.

Just who are these experts advising? Individuals and couples are subject to the top 35 percent tax rate only if they have taxable income of more than about $370,000 a year. Individuals hit the second highest rate, 33 percent, only if their taxable income tops about $170,000. For couples filing jointly it's about $210,000. (These were the numbers in 2009.)

Bluntly, if you are earning $370,000 a year in retirement you really don't have too much to worry about. If you are earning more than $210,000 a year as a couple—this is after deductions—you probably don't, either. The average married couple in retirement lives on about $31,000 a year, according to the U.S. Census. So they're going to pay only 15 percent tax on any income. Even a couple that earns $65,000 is going to pay only 15 percent.

If your ship comes in, yes, your tax rates will rise and you will keep less of the money you withdraw from your shelters. But you will need it less, too. However, if your ship doesn't come in, you will keep more.

Make the Most of Your 401(k)

If you can afford to, you should try to contribute as much as you can to your 401(k) plan—or the equivalent, such as a 457 or a 403(b)—at work. The money is deducted from your pay at the source, and that makes the saving automatic. Every time you choose to take a dollar as taxable income that you could have saved in your 401(k) instead, you are simply handing over free cash to the government.

Employers may limit your contribution to a certain percentage of your income. In 2009 the maximum contribution under law was $16,500 a year ($22,000 if you are over 50). Up to a certain level, your employer may match your contributions with a contribution of its own. So for the first $2,000 you put in, say, or the first 2 percent of your salary, your employer may add some of its own money. Such matching contributions are becoming rarer. But many employers still offer them. It really is free money. Not taking it is a sin. You are just throwing away cash.

Money you put into a 401(k) is deducted from your taxable income. If you are on track to report, say, $96,500 in taxable income next year, but you contribute the maximum $16,500 to your 401(k) plan instead, you only have to report $80,000 in taxable income.

If you are in a 25 percent federal tax bracket, that's a straight saving of $4,125 a year. Your 401(k), of course, will then grow tax deferred.

Money invested in a 401(k) is intended for retirement. You aren't supposed to touch it until you are 59½. You may be allowed to get your hands on your money early under certain conditions, usually associated with hardship. There are a few technical exceptions, but in most cases you will have to pay both income tax and a 10 percent penalty on any money you take out early. Don't contribute money to a 401(k) that you will need early.

The main problem with a 401(k) is that you are usually presented with limited investment options. The smart play is to use the best of what you are offered as part of your overall investment plan. Look first for low-cost TIPS or taxable bond funds, and then at low-cost general equity funds. In many cases, the higher-fee mutual funds that are offered won't be worth the extra fees.

Ironically, a 401(k) plan gets better when you leave your employer. Then you can roll it over into an IRA. Contact any reputable broker, who will handle it for you. Once you have rolled a plan over, you are suddenly free to invest the money in whatever you want.

Make the Most of Your IRA

You can also give yourself a big help with taxes, too, by making the full use of your IRA allowances each year. For 2009 the contribution limits were $5,000 a year ($6,000 if you are over 50). And couples get an extra break. If one spouse isn't working, the other can still give the nonworking spouse money to put into a spousal IRA.

There are three kinds of IRAs to choose from.

In a traditional IRA you contribute pretax dollars, but the money is taxed when you withdraw it. A Roth IRA, meanwhile, works the other way around. You contribute after-tax dollars, but the money is tax free when you take it out.

If you have modified adjusted gross income over $105,000, or $166,000 for couples filing jointly, you may not be allowed to contribute much, if anything, to either a traditional or a Roth IRA. That may leave you pondering a third, lesser alternative: the nondeductible traditional IRA. There are no income limits. Everyone qualifies.

You contribute after-tax dollars. And any profits are taxed when you withdraw them. During the boom, many tax advisers dismissed these. They said they weren't much good. They made little sense with stocks. But they still make sense for a lot of people for five other reasons.

1. They're still excellent for bonds.
2. Unlike with a 401(k), you have control over how to invest the money. You can, for example, buy a single 20-year TIPS bond to hold in an IRA.

3. They also shelter your money from creditors in the event of bankruptcy, just like any other IRA.
4. The money is invisible for student aid calculations.
5. As of this writing, the law provides a remarkable one-year loophole due to open in 2010 only. During that year anyone would be allowed to transfer assets from any other kind of IRA, including a nondeductible traditional IRA, into a Roth. This is a terrific back door into a Roth for people who earn too much to qualify normally. So someone over the income limit has yet another incentive to put the maximum into a nondeductible traditional IRA: They can transfer it into a Roth in due course.

Money in an IRA, like that in a 401(k) or equivalent, is intended for retirement. In most cases you're not supposed to touch it until you're 59½, and if you do you'll get hit with any income tax due plus a 10 percent penalty. But there are a few get-out clauses that escape the penalty, including using money for education or a first home purchase.

One that may be important in certain emergencies is called a substantially equal periodic payment (SEPP). We looked at this earlier, in relation to emergency lifelines. It's an important feature.

You can withdraw a certain amount per year without paying the penalty. There are complex technical ways of calculating how much you can withdraw. The payments will be based on your life expectancy and annuity tables. They need to be about the same each year for at least five years. You will need to talk to your IRA provider to organize it and make sure it complies with the rules. But it's important and useful to know this option is there if you need it. It's another advantage to IRAs.

Life Insurance and Variable Annuities

If you are running out of tax shelters, life insurance and variable annuities are also worth a look. They are a little-understood, and often overlooked, extra shelter.

Life insurance enjoys tax benefits. It can be a very tax-efficient way of estate planning, assuming the policy is owned and structured appropriately. Cash-value life insurance policies can also help you shelter retirement savings, too.

The problem, of course, is that they are often mediocre investments. As mentioned earlier, insurance products often involve high fees and rarely produce the best returns. But if you need to shelter more money from taxes, and perhaps from creditors, they may be worth a look.

One that can give you more control is a variable annuity. This is a form of investment account that is sheltered from taxes because it calls itself a life insurance policy. During the boom, variable annuities were downplayed for the usual reasons—everyone had all their money in lightly taxed stocks.

Variable annuities have frequently earned a terrible reputation for high fees, poor performance, and bad lock-in features. They often deserved it. But newer, lower-cost versions, from the likes of Vanguard, Charles Schwab, and Fidelity, are much better. The difference between bad variable annuities and the new low-cost ones is like night and day.

In a variable annuity, you contribute with after-tax dollars and withdraw the money as taxable income. So far, it may not sound appealing. But while the money is inside the variable annuity it is sheltered from annual investment taxes at the state and federal levels. You won't have to pay any capital gains tax, or dividend or ordinary income tax.

They are, of course, especially good for bonds, which would otherwise be taxed heavily.

You can save as much as you like in a variable annuity. Unlike the 401(k) and IRA shelters, there are no limits to what you can put in. You aren't dependent on your employer to choose the plan. You can go to any provider you want and choose your own options.

Money in a variable annuity may also be safe from creditors if financial disaster hits you. The rules vary from state to state.

When it comes time to retire, you can defer the eventual tax bill on your savings still further, by converting your annuity into one that pays out money until death. If necessary you can make a tax-free swap from one annuity to another, using a so-called 1035 exchange. (It's called that after the relevant section of the tax code.)

Either way, you won't have to pay any taxes until you receive the checks. As you could be receiving income for life, this means taxes on some of this money won't come due until your final days. And, of course, such taxes are progressive. The more you need the money, the lower your taxes, so the more of it you will get to keep.

Variable annuities are retirement vehicles. There are 10 percent penalties, as well as taxes, to pay on early withdrawals. They're not a good home for money you may need in the short term. But they may be useful as a shelter.

Self-Employed Shelters

If you are self-employed, or if you just have some extra income on the side, there are extra tax breaks for you. That's especially good news in a tough economy, when many people who lose their jobs may end up working for themselves.

There are special tax-deferred retirement accounts designed for people who are self-employed, including Keogh plans, self-employed pension individual retirement accounts (SEP-IRAs), and self-employed or solo 401(k) plans.

And they can be terrific deals. They can let you shelter 25 percent of your compensation up to $49,000, or $54,500 in the case of a solo 401(k) if you are over 50. There are, as usual, penalties on early withdrawals in most cases.

For those over 50 who have a lot of self-employed income, the really smart move can be to set up a personal pension. The federal government wants the self-employed to save as much as possible for their retirement, and it gives them incentives to match. Over 50, as retirement age looms, those become remarkably generous. You should talk directly to a pension expert, who can help set up a plan that may allow you to shelter even more of your income.

Shelters and College Savings

If you are struggling to save up money to help children or grand-children through college, take a look at 529 college savings plans as well.

These are special tax shelters specifically designed to help save for college tuition.

As we saw earlier, college costs have been rising sharply for years. Four years at your typical State U now costs about $42,000. A private college typically costs more than twice that. College savings 529 plans can help.

The money will grow faster because in a 529 it is sheltered from all investment taxes. As long as the money is withdrawn only for qualified college costs, like tuition, it can be withdrawn tax-free as well. In some states there's a final bonus: You may also deduct some of your contributions from your taxable income.

The money may also be protected from creditors. The 2005 bankruptcy law protects your 529 plans from creditors if you hold the plans for direct descendants—children, grandchildren, or step-children or step-grandchildren. There is a wrinkle. Under the federal rules, you can't throw all your money into a 529 plan shortly before filing for bankruptcy. Money invested in a 529 plan more than two years before filing is secure. Another $5,000 invested more than one year before filing is also secure. But money invested during the year before filing for bankruptcy isn't secure. Your state may offer additional protection.

Setting up a plan can help you, and everyone in your circle, focus on the challenge of saving up to send your children to college. It can also help focus, and maybe even motivate, your children. People often have no idea what to buy children for Christmas and birthdays. That's especially true for friends and more distant relatives. That present-buying desperation often begins when the children are newborns and continues when they are teenagers. During the age of easy money, people figured it didn't matter so much. They'd just take their best shot at a gift. If the money was wasted, well, it was only $30 or $50 or whatever.

Today, money is scarce and precious. But you can tell family and friends about your children's 529 accounts, and encourage them to give money.

You're more likely to ask them if you've set up a plan. And they're much more likely to give. In fact, they are more likely to be generous, as they know where the money is going. Every bit helps. Nobody knows what to give a baby. But $100 invested then should be worth at least $200 in inflation-adjusted terms by the time the child turns 18.

The tax rules regarding 529 plans are extremely good. You can open a separate 529 plan for each of your children. And you and your spouse can invest as much as $130,000 in each one straight-away, if you want to, without triggering any gift tax consequences. That's unique. Normally, the pair of you would only be allowed to give $26,000 to any individual before you had to file a gift tax return. But if it's a 529 plan for your children, Uncle Sam lets you use five years' worth of gift tax limits at once.

If you are worried that Junior or Missy is going to take the money, run away to India, and join a cult, relax. In a 529 plan, you keep control of the money, which means you can change the beneficiaries to another family member if you want.

And if you worry that the money you put in is going to hinder your children's chances of getting financial aid, you can relax about that, too. When it comes time to apply, the assets count as yours, not your child's. That's a big help, too. The financial aid formulas count 20 percent of students' own assets against their eligibility, but only 5.6 percent of yours.

As with most tax shelters, you face potential penalties for early or nonqualified withdrawals from a 529 plan. That means that if you take the money out without spending it on qualified tuition costs, you will face taxes plus a 10 percent penalty on any gains the money made in the account.

There's a pretty broad range of 529 plans to choose from. An oddity of 529s is that each plan has to be approved by the government of one of the 50 states, yet you are not restricted to the plans approved by your home state. Florida residents can sign up for one of the Nebraska plans if they want.

Look for a plan that offers good investment choices and low costs. Savingforcollege.com is a good source for more information.

Your choice isn't carved in stone. If you are unhappy with a plan, you can always swap at a later date into one of the alternatives. As long as you do it correctly, there will be no taxes to pay on the transfer. The simplest way to do that is through a direct rollover. Call the people who run the plan you want to get into, and tell them you want to do a direct rollover from your old plan. They should do all the paperwork for you.

There is a further tax bonus.

If your 529 investments prosper and rise in value, your gains are sheltered from federal taxes. But if you lose money, you can actually claim those losses on your federal tax return and use them to offset other taxable gains.

Heads you win, tails they lose.

To claim the losses for tax purposes, you would have to close the plan and withdraw the money. There are no taxes or penalties to pay, because those would apply only to your gains—and in this case there aren't any.

Instead, the losses can be used to offset any other capital gains you made on any other, taxable investments. If you have any losses left over after that, you can use $3,000 worth of them to offset taxable income. And if you still have losses left over after that, you can carry them forward until the following year.

If you want, after 61 days you can reinvest the money in a new 529 plan. But be sure to wait the full 61 days before you do. Otherwise the IRS won't consider this a withdrawal. The IRS will consider it an indirect rollover from the old plan to the new one. You won't get the tax benefit from the loss. Check with the operator of your new plan to make sure you handle the transfer properly.

There is one caveat. Once you have made that withdrawal, putting the money back into another 529 plan will constitute a completely new gift, with potential gift tax consequences.

As ever, you will have to do your own math. If your 529 plan has lost only a small amount of money, this procedure may not be worth it. But if you have big losses, and especially if you are facing big capital gains elsewhere in your portfolio, the math may be compelling.

Those saving for college should also look at Coverdell Education Savings Accounts. Those are another type of tax shelter for education savings. They work a little bit like a Roth IRA—the money goes in after tax, but comes out tax free. However, they are much less appealing than a 529 plan. The contribution limit is just $2,500 and there are eligibility restrictions.

Make the Most of Your Investment Losses

If you have lost money on shares, don't despair completely. You can at least put those losses to work for you by harvesting them to lower your taxes.

Sophisticated investors already work the IRS rules to do this every year. Everyone should do it.

Tax loss harvesting means selling shares on which you have lost money. (If you still like the stocks, you must wait at least 31 days before buying them back again.)

Once you do this you can claim the losses on your tax returns. You can use them to offset any capital gains, and any left over can offset up to $3,000 in earned income. And if this process still leaves you with losses left over, you can carry them forward to future years—when you can use them to shelter further capital gains or further taxable income.

Tax loss harvesting is common during a boom. It's even more valuable in a slump. That's because when the losses are greater than the capital gains, you get to use them to offset taxable income. And that's probably going to save a lot of people more money, because income is generally taxed at higher rates than long-term capital gains.

If an investor sells the shares but buys them back within 31 days, the IRS won't recognize the sale. You need to stay out of the stock completely. The problem? The market, and your stock, could turn around in that month and rise a long way. By the time you're able to buy back in, you may have missed the rise.

There is a workaround. You can sell the stock and put the money in an exchange-traded fund that tracks the same sector.

So if you've lost money on shares in a major technology company, you can sell it to book the tax loss and keep the money for 31 days in an exchange-traded fund that tracks the technology sector. If you've lost money on a leading pharmaceuticals stock, you can do the same with a fund that tracks the pharmaceutical industry.

Under the tax laws, that's okay. As long as you don't invest in the same or a "substantially identical" security, you're fine.

The workaround isn't perfect. If it were, the IRS wouldn't allow it. So it's still possible that the stock you sold will rise while the rest of its sector doesn't. In that case you've missed out on the gains, while the exchange-traded fund you bought either goes nowhere or even falls. This is much more likely with a smaller company stock or one that is atypical for its industry. But this maneuver does significantly reduce your risk. Oftentimes a stock is down because the industry is in free fall. Any burst of good news or market optimism that causes one leading stock to rally is probably going to lift its peers as well.

How Not to Lose Everything

Bad things happen to good people. At one point 20,000 Americans were filing for bankruptcy each week. If you are deeply in debt and cannot find a way out, you may want to consider it.

Bankruptcy is a legal process that can wipe out your debts and give you something close to a fresh start. The main form is known as Chapter 7. (There is also another type of bankruptcy, known as Chapter 13, that gives you lesser relief. It structures repayments over time.) Bankruptcy will certainly hit your credit score. That, of course, is likely to affect your ability to get new credit, including a mortgage. But if you are contemplating bankruptcy, your credit score is probably poor already. Ironically, by giving you a fresh start, bankruptcy may help you rebuild your score more quickly. Chapter 7 bankruptcy will be wiped off your credit report after 10 years.

If you think you are heading toward a possible bankruptcy, you should get help quickly. For a credit counselor, the U.S. Trustees, a branch of the Department of Justice that deals with bankruptcy, maintains a database of agencies. The National Foundation for Credit Counseling, a nationwide organization that has been around since 1951, can also help you locate a counselor in your area. They can be found at www.nfcc.org, and they have a consumer hotline at 1-800-388-2227. Other sources include NeighborWorks America, a national nonprofit that was set up by Congress in 1978 and is focused on local housing issues. If you are looking for a bankruptcy attorney who can help guide you through the process, the American Bankruptcy Institute (www.abiworld.org) and the National Association of Consumer Bankruptcy Attorneys (www.nacba.org) may be able to help you find a specialist in your area.

Once you start the process of filing for bankruptcy, options start closing for you. It generally becomes too late to take many of the key steps to protect what you still have. Your adviser or counselor can give you specific advice. The smart move is to act earlier to shelter what you can. Keep contributing to your retirement plans if you can. Money in a qualified pension plan or held in a 401(k) or equivalent, like a 403(b), is sheltered from creditors, even in bankruptcy. That's also true for money in an individual retirement account (IRA), up to $1 million.

As mentioned earlier, money in 529 college savings plans for your children is also protected from creditors—if you make the contributions early enough. Under the new bankruptcy law passed in 2005, anything that has been in a 529 for at least two years is safe, and another $5,000 that's been inside for at least one year is safe as well. Your state may offer further protection.

Other states offer other shelters as well. They can include life insurance policies and variable annuities. It depends on which state you live in. A few years ago a man in Iowa realized he was heading for bankruptcy and looked up the relevant laws in his state. The family shotgun counts as sheltered property there. So he rushed out and spent $10,000 of his spare cash on a rare and valuable gun, simply to protect the money. The judge backed him up, too. He said he wasn't there to second-guess the reason for the law. (The man in question was lucky. In most cases judges overturn last-minute moves like this that are an obvious dodge.)

You can often protect your home as well. You can't easily protect it if you default on your mortgage. After all, that's a loan secured against the property. (That's why you may be taking a risk by paying off credit cards with a refinanced mortgage or a home equity loan.) But in many states it's easy to protect it from everyone else. How to do this depends on where you live. Your primary residence, known as your homestead, often enjoys considerable security against creditors under law. Florida and Texas are the states with the most generous rules. Their so-called homestead exemptions are effectively limitless, although following the 2005 change in the bankruptcy law someone needs to live there for two years to enjoy the full benefits. Most states offer at least some homestead protection. Taking advantage is often as simple as filing a form declaring the home your homestead.

In some states, married couples have another, little-known option: owning their home as tenants by the entirety. This is a legal form available only to married couples. What it means, in layman's terms, is that the home is no longer owned by either the husband or the wife. It is effectively owned by the marriage. So only a creditor with a claim against both spouses is going to have an easy task going after their home equity. But be aware there are wrinkles from state to state.

Nobody with any sense wants to end up in bankruptcy. But if you have behaved responsibly and been hit with bad luck, don't feel too bad about it. No one ever wants to admit this, but walking away from debts is as American as apple pie. That is, after all, one of the main reasons for the foundation stone of the capitalist system—the incorporated business. It means the people who own a company, whether they be Lehman Brothers stockholders or your dry cleaner, have limited liability. They can pocket all the profits on the way up, without having to pay a penny of that back to creditors if things go wrong.

Shareholders in Washington Mutual collected about $6 billion in dividends in the three years before the bank collapsed in September 2008. They can spend that money on speedboats and champagne—it's all theirs. Six top executives at Lehman Brothers shared $116 million in cash in the three years before their bank imploded. They nearly brought down the capitalist system, but they kept the loot. It's the same every time a company collapses. Personal bankruptcy is just the bailout for the common man (and woman).

Remember, too, that the banks didn't have to lend to you. They knew what they were doing. Those loans were big business for a good time. And the stockholders were happy.

Conclusion

Don't neglect tax shelters in a turbulent economy. When times are tough, too many people make the mistake of downplaying the importance of tax shelters. It's hard to think about sheltering your investments from future taxes at a time when they are a sea of red ink. And you may not want to lock money away when the present is so unsettled. Nonetheless, shelters are a valuable break that's available to the ordinary public. They are more important, not less important, during turbulent times. They let you increase the returns on your investments by cutting the taxes you pay. They are especially good for sheltering bonds. And they are shelters from creditors as well as from Uncle Sam. It makes sense to get the most out of the shelters available to you.

CHAPTER

Next Steps

A plan is useful only if you put it into practice. In this final chapter we'll look at three things.

We'll recap the key points of the plan. We'll take a closer look at some of the core themes involved in protecting your finances and building your wealth. And then we'll take a look at how to get started and begin putting some of these ideas into practice.

Checking the Map

- Many people are unprepared for the future. Retirement will likely last much longer, and cost much more, than you may realize. You may live for 30 or 40 years after you turn 65.
- To build a plan, you should select your destination, work out where you are now, and then find the route.
- Start by working out how much retirement income you will need. A rule of thumb says you may need 75 percent of what you earn now.
- Deduct your likely annual Social Security and pension. What's left over is what you will need to provide yourself. You should aim to save about 20 times that amount.
- From this you can work out an annual savings target that will get you back on track.
- Too many people think a booming stock market is going to bail them out. Returns are probably going to be far less than hoped. For many that means having to save more.

177

- If the targets look too high, you can help by scaling back your goals, delaying them, or rethinking your legacy and buying an annuity.

The Basics

- Pay off those credit cards. It's the most powerful thing you can do for your finances. Until you do, you're going backwards financially.
- Secure your financial lifelines. You should be able to get your hands on several months' worth of expenses in case of emergency.
- Bank accounts are poor long-term homes for your money. Consider other options, including bonds, especially tax-free municipals, which may earn a higher return. You should also look to tap emergency loans, such as a home equity line of credit. Only use credit card debt in dire emergencies.
- Check your insurance coverage. Make sure you are protected against major risks. This includes making sure you have the life, disability, liability, and long-term care insurance you need.
- Also check the claim limits, and any gaps, on your homeowners' policy and ensure you have an up-to-date inventory of your possessions.

How Not to Invest

- There are no simplistic investment rules that will magically produce superior returns.
- Shares are not the miraculous investments their cheerleaders claim. The returns may be significantly lower than so many expect. Traditional diversification strategies and regular mutual funds may not protect you as much as you think.
- Investing in your own employer is incredibly risky. You already have a big investment in the company: You work there.
- Neither bank accounts nor bonds are riskless, either. They are vulnerable to inflation and taxes, and in the case of some bonds, to default risk as well.

- Gold and real estate also come with risks. They are more volatile than many realize, and their long-term returns may be overstated.

Storm Proof Your Portfolio

- The future is uncertain, so the most secure portfolio is braced for many eventualities. True diversification involves genuinely different investments that will perform differently.
- That can include inflation-protected government bonds, global stock market index funds, and flexible, smart funds that can adapt to events and pursue different strategies.
- Those smart funds can include asset allocation, long-short, and maverick mutual funds. Each type is different and offers different strengths and risks.
- Other options include covered calls, precious metals, and bond funds.
- Closed-end funds can offer opportunities for private investors when they are trading at a big discount to their underlying net worth.
- The safest way to invest in the stock market is little and often, using dollar-cost averaging to smooth your returns.
- It's hard not to panic in a crash, but it's worth remembering that these are times to buy, not to sell. The world hasn't ended yet.
- If your compensation includes a lot of company stock or options, you might want to consider using derivatives to try to hedge and protect yourself from a collapse.

Cash Flow Positive from Right Now

- The sticker price on an item you buy is only one of your costs—and it's the least important.
- The opportunity cost of the money you spend is far greater. Each dollar you spend may actually cost you another $3 or $4 in hidden cost.
- The second set of costs consists of repeat costs. Over time they, too, dwarf the sticker price.

- Put the opportunity and repeat costs together and the results are explosive: $1 a month over 35 years will end up costing you $1,000—after adjusting for inflation.
- So if you can recapture $500 a month of those costs, you can save $500,000 over time with remarkably little sacrifice.

Cover Your Assets

- Tax shelters are more important than every before.
- They are sheltered from creditors as well as taxes.
- They are great for bonds.
- Taxes are likely to rise.
- Tax shelters help your children qualify for financial aid when they apply to college.
- And they are progressive—tax shelters pay out more the more you need them.
- You should definitely make the most of your 401(k) or equivalent—like a 403(b)—at work and your IRA. Variable annuities can offer further shelter if you need it.
- There are great tax breaks available to you if you are self-employed, or have a second income as an independent contractor.
- And 529 plans can be valuable both as college savings plans and as shelters.
- Make sure to harvest any tax losses to offset more taxes.
- And if you get into serious trouble, be aware that bankruptcy is a serious option. If you act intelligently and plan ahead, you may be able to protect most, or all, of what you own.

The Principles of Storm Proofing

It's not just about the details. Too much financial advice is buried in the nitty-gritty. Yes, you can talk about this mutual fund or that tax shelter. But the really important messages cut across many different topics. They are broad principles, or themes, that run through everything.

What are they?

There is no holy grail of investing. There is no alchemy that will turn lead into gold. If there were a guaranteed way to beat the market, everyone would soon discover it—and then who would be left behind to underperform the market? And if someone really had discovered it, do you think he would be an ex-Jacuzzi salesman managing money for your brother-in-law, or he would be giving seminars at the airport Marriott?

Good defense beats good offense. Someone investing in the stock market would do extremely well to make 14 percent a year. Few will achieve it. Anyone with a balance on their credit card can earn that kind of return, with absolutely no risk at all, by paying off the card. But instead they are often out looking for the hot tip that will somehow save them.

Dull investing beats exciting investing. I've met some very rich investors. They all made their money the boring way—doing their homework, studying fundamentals, and being patient. All of them. I've also met lots of people who trade on the basis of hot tips, rumors, and the next big thing. They are all still working for somebody else.

It's all about cash flow. You are either earning cash or you are burning cash. There is, alas, no third alternative for those who feel they are getting by but haven't checked the books lately. Nor for those who have borrowed money against a home that went up recently. Bottom line: Every week, month, and year, money came in and money went out. One number is always bigger than the other. And if it's the second one, you're going backwards.

In England this is known as "Micawberism," after Wilkins Micawber, a character in Charles Dickens's *David Copperfield.* Mr. Micawber noted that if money in beat money out, even by a penny, the result was financial happiness. If the reverse: misery. It's easy to satirize, but impossible to refute.

Life is longer than you think. If you live a full span of years, you may live for 30 or even 40 years after you turn 65. Most people aren't prepared. That third stage of life will be very different for those who have prepared and saved for it and for those who haven't.

It's a marathon, not a sprint. When it comes to investing, your greatest ally isn't a broker with hot tips or some system you heard about on TV. It's time. The stock market, jokes Warren Buffett, is a mechanism for distributing wealth from the active to the patient.

Over long periods, regular and steady returns will build a lot of wealth.

Hope for the best, but plan for the worst. The problem with the *Titanic* wasn't that the owners thought the ship was safe. It was that they didn't order enough lifeboats for everyone on board. There's nothing wrong with hoping the stock market will go up 10 percent a year. Maybe it will. The mistake for the past 20 years has been planning on it.

You have to take charge of your own finances. No one else can take responsibility. No one is going to care as much as you. Even if you have an adviser you trust, you will be in a far stronger position if you take time to understand what the adviser is doing and why. As the discount clothing chain Syms likes to say, an educated consumer is the best customer.

Many professional advisers, such as lawyers and accountants, are better at answering focused questions than they are at volunteering solutions. If you know the questions to ask and the ideas to suggest, you will probably find they add much more value.

Don't underestimate a dollar. Our grandparents used to say, "A penny saved is a penny earned." But they were lowballing it. You probably have to earn $1.25 or more to put a dollar in your pocket, because you will have to pay taxes. Money saved is tax free. And of course we all tend to underestimate those two big extra costs: opportunity (or hidden) cost and repeat cost. A dollar saved is really $4 or more over time. A dollar saved every month will eventually be worth $1,000. If you are currently contributing less than the maximum to your 401(k) plan at work, the numbers are remarkable. Save that dollar a month, and contribute it to your plan, and you will effectively get back the income tax you would have paid on it. So the dollar becomes maybe $1.25, and over many decades should grow into about $1,250 or more. In today's money.

Staying on Track

All plans need constant adjustments. You have to keep checking the map and where you are.

Take time regularly to check on your progress, and make changes if you get off course.

Life has a habit of getting in the way. It's so easy to get too busy and put financial issues on the back burner. So give thought to a system of regular reviews that will work for you.

If you can, review your budget at least once a quarter. Look at your spending over the quarter and how your financial position has changed from three months earlier. At the very least, check your bank accounts regularly. See where you are going off the plan and take steps to get back onto it.

Look at your investments regularly as well. Do take time to understand what your fund managers are doing, and why. An educated investor is the best investor. Thanks to the Internet, it is easier than ever to gain the knowledge you need about markets, strategies, and your money.

Don't panic too much about short-term moves in the markets. If you have the right investments, you will weather them.

It's a good idea to consider reviewing your portfolio at least once a year to see if it needs rebalancing. At times some investments will do better than others, so they will grow to become a bigger part of your portfolio by value than you originally intended. Rebalancing involves shifting money between them to bring their weightings back into line.

The kind of smart, flexible funds we looked at earlier do some of this rebalancing themselves. Any good smart fund manager is likely to respond to a boom in one area and a slump in another by shifting money from one to the other. Yet the portfolio will still need adjusting. In particular, a maverick fund manager who has just had a terrific run may therefore be managing more of your money than is prudent.

Getting Started

Finally, the best plan is worthless if you don't put it into practice. You'll make a difference to your life only if you act.

Wondering where to start? Start anywhere.

Don't just stand there. Do something!

Sit down and review your destination: your retirement goal, or your college savings target.

Or walk into a local branch of Schwab, Fidelity, or the like and open up an IRA for this year. Or contact human resources at work to find out about opening up a 401(k) plan. Or, if you have one, find out whether you can raise your contributions.

Start researching competitive insurance rates to see if you can save money on your home or car insurance.

Or review your investment portfolio and start making changes. It's hard to view your investment strategy clearly through the detritus of your current portfolio. If your investments are in tax shelters, you can generate some momentum just by selling those mediocre old McMoney mutual funds you own. And those speculative stocks you bought on someone's recommendation that have gone nowhere—or down.

If you wouldn't buy an investment now, you shouldn't own it now. Hanging on to something you bought in the past makes no sense. Sure, it might go up tomorrow. But so might something else.

Obviously, if your investments are held outside a tax shelter, you may have tax consequences if you sell. But don't let that rule you completely. The wrong investments will end up costing you a lot more than taxes.

Looking for other ideas to get you started? Call up your cell phone company and threaten to leave. Cancel your landline. Check your local credit union and see if it will give you a better deal than your present bank.

Buy a bread maker and start making your own bread. Buy a cappuccino machine.

Go online and find coupon deals for your groceries. Start clipping them out. Next time you go to the store, buy some no-brand products. Remember that every dollar you save may end up saving you $4, and every dollar you save a month may end up saving you $1,000.

Cancel cable until you pay off your credit card. Make your own lunch tomorrow. Buy a Thermos. Leave your cards at home and start carrying cash.

Your biggest enemies are inertia and procrastination. The only way to get started is to get started. Good luck!

Appendix
Investment Spotlight

This appendix highlights 17 types of investment themes—ideas and pitfalls—to help show how you can evaluate new opportunities. They include:

1. Tobacco
2. Diageo
3. Amazon
4. Fad stocks
5. Share spike 1: the fake present tense
6. Sheltering bonds
7. Share spike 2: jumping on at the peak
8. Bread maker
9. Inflation
10. Dollar a month
11. TIPS versus cash
12. TIPS over 2 percent
13. TIPS yields by maturity
14. Hourly rates
15. Junk
16. Yield curve
17. $100 over 35 years

Tobacco

It's hard enough to beat the market. Few will succeed. But it may be a little easier if you focus on the one thing that really matters: cash flow. Few industries have ever become as unfashionable as quickly as big tobacco has over the past 25 years. In the mid-1980s people could still smoke in the office and on planes. Cigarettes are a dying industry (literally as well as figuratively). But the cash flow has been immense. The stocks pay enormous dividends. An investor who held only tobacco stocks over that time would have left the rest of the stock market far behind, even though the industry was deeply unfashionable and is in terminal decline. (See Figure A.1.)

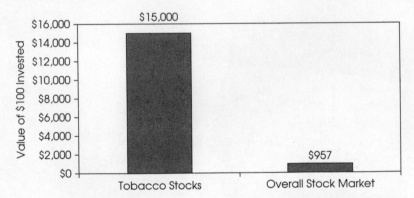

Figure A.1   Value of $100 Invested in Tobacco versus the Overall Stock Market, 1985 to 2009

Data source: Copyright 2009 FactSet Research Systems Inc. All rights reserved.

Diageo

The best investments are often the ones nobody is talking about. At the height of the dot-com mania, early in 2000, everyone was trying to find the next hot Internet stock. It was a great time to invest . . . in the old economy stocks that nobody wanted. Diageo, formerly known as Guinness, is the world's largest liquor company. In addition to Guinness beer, it makes Smirnoff vodka, Captain Morgan rum, Bailey's Irish Cream, lots of Scotch whiskys, and various other drinks. It may not be the next big thing, but it is a highly profitable cash machine. In early 2000, as investors chased high-tech dreams, stocks like this got thrown overboard. Someone who invested $100 in Diageo then and just held on, reinvesting the dividends, would have had about $250 by 2009—even while the overall stock market fell. (See Figure A.2.)

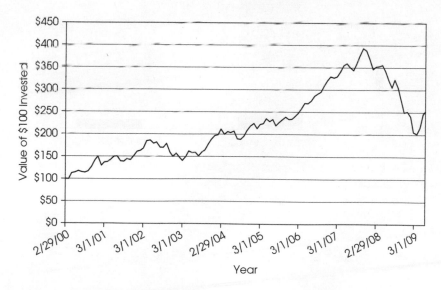

Figure A.2   Value of $100 Invested in Diageo, with Dividends Reinvested, 2000 to 2009

Data source: Copyright 2009 FactSet Research Systems Inc. All rights reserved.

Amazon

Never pay too much for a stock. In the 10 years after the dot-com bubble, Amazon.com has done pretty much everything its fans might have hoped for. It boosted sales more than tenfold, became a powerful worldwide company, revolutionized retailing, and transformed its bottom line from about $600 billion in losses in 1999 to nearly $1 billion in pretax profits in 2008. Yet investors who anticipated all of this business success, but who foolishly overpaid for the stock at the peak, got no reward for their foresight. By 2009 the shares had barely recovered their earlier peak—after suffering years of red ink and misery. (See Figure A.3.) These investors would have been far better off holding their money in, say, municipal bonds.

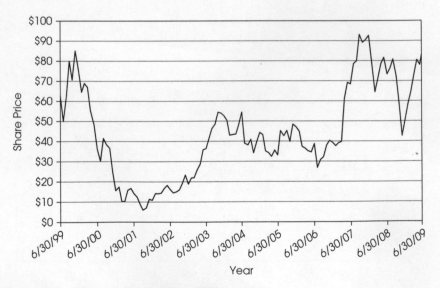

Figure A.3   Amazon Stock Price, 1999 to 2009

Fad Stocks

Beware fad stocks!

Wall Street is like a teenager. It falls in love easily, chases every new fad, and it never cleans up after itself. So look out for the fashion—or crush—of the moment. Remember Netscape? Krispy Kreme Donuts (see Figure A.4)? XM Satellite Radio? The sky was the limit—then they crashed. There's often a hot stock of the moment that everybody absolutely has to own. There's usually a seductive story line to justify its soaring share price ("There's a billion people in China. If they all buy this widget, this company will be making . . ."). And no matter how high it rises, there will always be experts who think it will still go higher. By the time you've heard about it, it is probably too late. Few fortunes have been made by jumping on these bandwagons, but plenty have been lost.

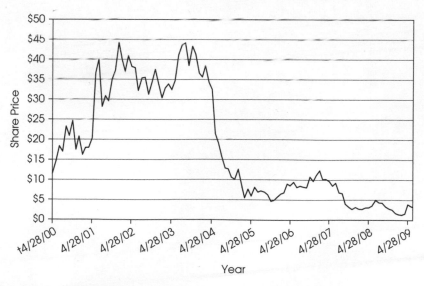

Figure A.4   Krispy Kreme Stock Price, 2000 to 2009

Share Spike 1: The Fake Present Tense

Does the stock shown in Figure A.5 look like a good investment? A lot of people will look at this graph and think it must be. "Look," they'll say. "It's going through the roof!" Beware the fake present tense. What they really mean, of course, is simply that the share *has-gone* through the roof. Unless you have a time machine, such information is of no use. And the rise leaves the shares correspondingly expensive. Want to see what this share was, and what happened next? Look at Figure A.7 on page 192.

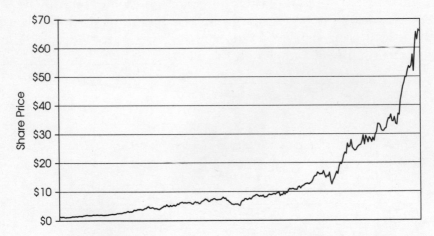

Figure A.5   Does This Share Look Like a Good Investment?
Data source: Copyright 2009 FactSet Research Systems Inc. All rights reserved.

Sheltering Bonds

Tax shelters are especially important for holding bonds, because otherwise their coupons will count as taxable income each year. In the case of inflation-protected TIPS bonds, that will also be true for the twice-yearly technical adjustments to the principal to reflect inflation. Consider someone who invests $10,000 in 30-year bonds paying 6 percent interest. If they hold the bonds in taxable accounts and pay 25 percent income tax each year, after 30 years they'll have about $37,453. But if they keep the bonds in a shelter they'll have $20,000 more. (See Figure A.6.)

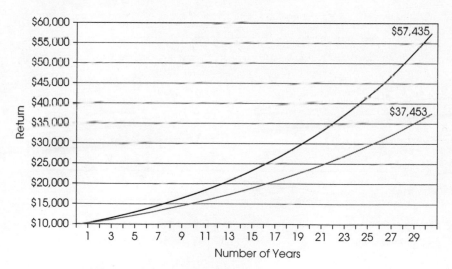

Figure A.6 Why You Should Shelter Bonds

Share Spike 2: Jumping On at the Peak

The company was Cisco Systems, a leading technology company, and the chart in Figure A.7 shows its share price rocketing up until March 2000. At that point it was the world's most valuable company by market value. Although Cisco was a high-quality company that played a key role in building out the Internet, the shares could not support anything like the price investors were paying. They collapsed until stabilizing a year later. The company remains in business and sales have grown, but those who jumped on board at the peak lost a lot of money nonetheless.

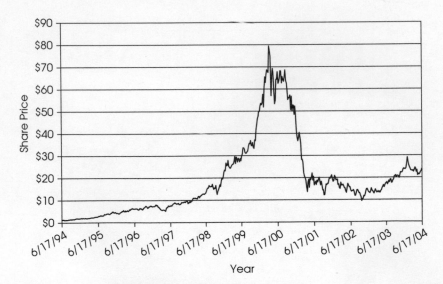

Figure A.7   Cisco Systems Share Price, 1994 to 2004

Bread Maker

Figure A.8 shows annualized returns comparing Microsoft, Wall Street in 1915, and a bread maker.

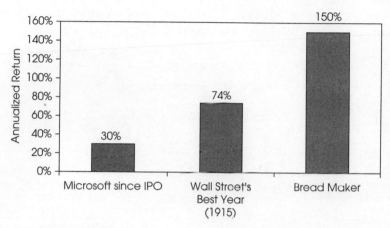

Figure A.8   Annualized Returns

Inflation

Not even your mattress—or a bank account—is a completely safe place to keep your money. Inflation is a silent but deadly killer of wealth. Look at how the real value of $1—in other words, the purchasing power—has declined over the past century, as shown in Figure A.9. Since 1913, a dollar has lost 95 percent of its value.

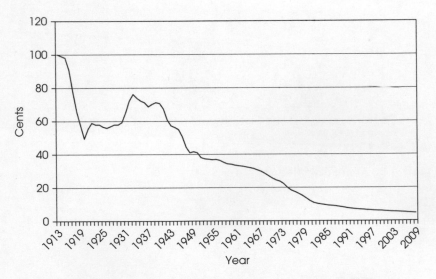

Figure A.9   Shrinking Value of a Dollar in Real Terms, 1913 to 2008
Data source: U.S. Department of Labor.

Dollar a Month

Figure A.10 shows the value of saving $1 a month over time.

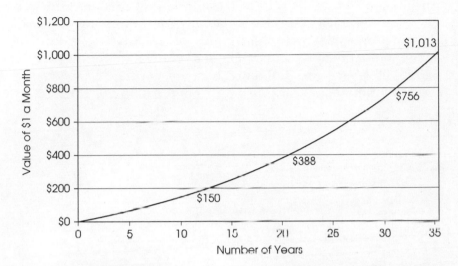

Figure A.10   Value of Saving $1 a Month (at 4.5 Percent Interest) over 10, 20, 30, and 35 Years

TIPS versus Cash

Savers who are afraid of risk try to keep their money safe in bank accounts. It's a false security. The interest barely keeps pace with inflation. From 1966 to 2008, money kept in short-term certificates of deposit (CDs) beat inflation by just 0.5 percent a year. Inflation-protected government bonds or TIPS, which also offer long-term security, also tend to offer better long-term returns as well. Figure A.11 shows the difference between earning 2.5 percent a year over inflation and earning only 0.5 percent for 20 years.

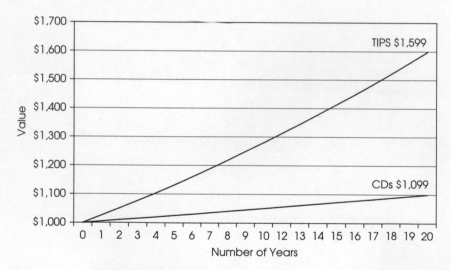

Figure A.11   Inflation-Protected Bonds versus CDs

TIPS over 2 Percent

The real or after-inflation yield on TIPS varies depending on the market. The higher it is when you buy the bond, the better. A real yield over 2 percent is usually a decent deal. Anything over 2.5 percent is pretty good. Those who bought 10-year TIPS with a real yield of less than 1 percent, in early 2008, got poor value. They would have done much better if they had waited a few months. (See Figure A.12.)

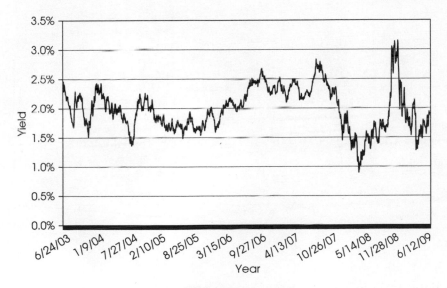

Figure A.12   Real Yield, 10-Year TIPS, 2003 to 2009
Data source: U.S. Treasury.

TIPS Yields by Maturity

TIPS that mature in 10 or even 20 years' time might fluctuate more in price at times, but they tend to pay much higher interest rates, as shown in Figure A.13. The returns may not compete with the stock market, but they come with no real risk. Note that these interest rates are on top of inflation.

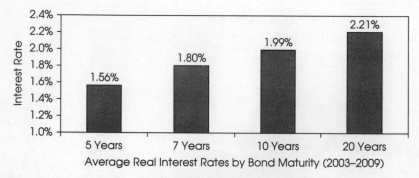

Figure A.13   Longer-Dated TIPS Bonds Tend to Pay Higher Interest

Hourly Rates

Just trying to save money isn't very helpful. One of the smartest things you can do is to value your time. Convert money-saving tasks into an hourly wage: It will give you a better idea of whether it's worth it. If it takes you five minutes to make lunch for work and it saves you a $6 purchase, that's the equivalent of earning $72 an hour—tax free. Add in the taxes, and you might have to earn about $96 an hour—or more—in paid work to do better. The average wage: $19 an hour. (See Figure A.14.) And yet the sandwich bars are filled every day with people who haven't done the math.

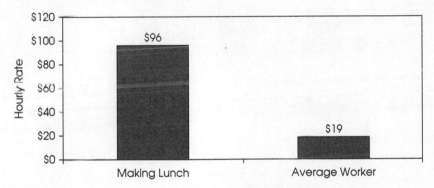

Figure A.14   Hourly Rates: Making Lunch versus Average Worker
Data source: U.S. Department of Labor.

Junk

When is junk not junk? So-called high-yield or junk bonds are those issued by riskier or more speculative companies. Conventional wisdom says they are risky investments. But it's not that simple. Any individual bond involves a lot of risk—if the company defaults, you may lose your entire investment. But a broadly based fund that holds many different high-yield bonds is much less risky. Many, maybe even most, of the bonds will work out fine—and they will pay handsomely. A high-yield bond fund can be a good bargain during financial panics, when such bonds tend to be very cheap. The crises of 2002 and 2008–2009 were great times to invest in a high-yield bond fund. (See Figure A.15.)

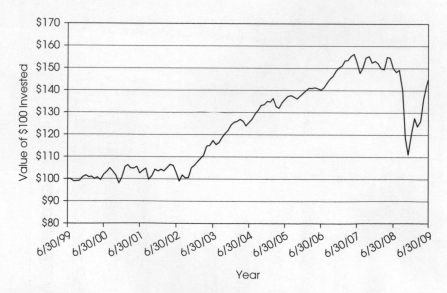

Figure A.15   Value of $100 Invested in the Vanguard High-Yield Bond Fund, 1999 to 2009

Yield Curve

Talk to any normal person about the Treasury yield curve and their eyes will glaze over like crockery. Wall Street loves to hide simple concepts behind jargon, because it helps them charge you more. The so-called yield curve is simply a way of comparing long-term government bond interest rates with short-term interest rates. A sample, from the end of 2007, can be seen in Figure A.16. Someone lending money to Uncle Sam for one year, by purchasing a one-year Treasury security, would have received 3.31 percent interest. Someone lending money to Uncle Sam for 30 years would have received 4.58 percent a year. You tend to get a higher rate of interest if you buy longer-term bonds because you are taking on more risk: If inflation picks up, your bonds may fall in value and the coupon payments will lose purchasing power. Personally, I'd buy long-term bonds only if they paid a lot more interest than short-term bonds. I like to be well compensated for any risks I take with my money.

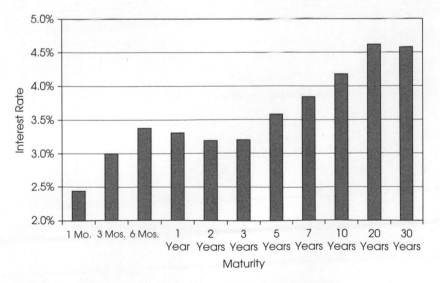

Figure A.16   Treasury Security Interest Rates, Year-End 2007
Data source: U.S. Treasury.

$100 over 35 Years

Compound interest and time are a powerful combination. Over 35 years, money invested at 4.5 percent above inflation will more than quadruple in value. (See Figure A.17.) Another way to look at the same fact: Every time you spend a dollar, you are actually taking about $4 out of your retirement account to do so.

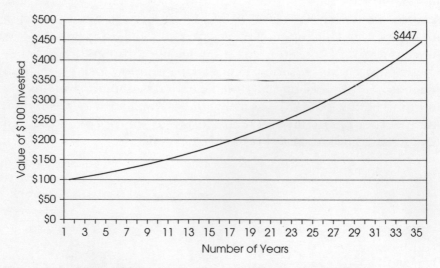

Figure A.17   Value of $100 Invested over 35 Years at 4.5 Percent

Index

A

AIG, 68
American Bankruptcy
 Institute, 173
Analysts, unreliability of, 50–51
Annuities, immediate, 27
Annuities, variable, 166–168
Apple, Inc., 65–66, 144

B

Babylon, Ancient, 74
Banking, online, 140
Bankruptcy, 32, 41–42, 173–175
Banks, fees, 139–140
Bank stocks, 50
Barrick Gold, 111
Bear markets, 52–53, 121–123
Bear Stearns, 57, 68
Beauty treatments, true cost of,
 137, 153
BlackRock, 95, 120
Bonds:
 corporate, 112, 115
 foreign, 85, 113–115
 funds, 116
 high-yield, 115–116
 inflation-protected, foreign, 85
 inflation-protected (TIPS),
  84–87, 105, 121, 162

municipal, 39–40, 115, 116–118
Treasury, 112
yields, 114
Boston Center for Retirement
 Studies, 90
Boston Herald, 51
Brands, cost of, 152
Bread makers, 133, 153–154
Brock, Fred, *How to Retire on Less
 Than You Think*, 23
Buffalo, American, 73
Buffett, Warren, 52, 57, 101–103
Business School, London, 49

C

Cable TV, costs, 144
Callan Associates, 106
Car, costs of owning, 134,
 156–157
Case, Professor Karl, 80
Cash, 58–59, 69–71, 145
Cash, risks of, 69–71, 81
Cell phones, cost, 145
Chernow, Ron, 124
Chicago Board Options
 Exchange, 106
Christmas, cost, 148–150
Cisco Systems, 10, 57
Citigroup, 68

Clews, Henry (nineteenth
  century financier), 124
College:
  costs, 16–17, 21
  savings, 16–17, 22, 163, 168–171
Commodities, 96
Contrarian investing, 51
Cost of living, U.S. cities, 23
Costs, opportunity, 130–132
Costs, repeat, 132–135
Coupons, 137, 143, 152
Covered calls, 128
Cramer, Jim, 65
Crashes, stock market, 90, 120–126
Credit cards, 4, 31–36, 41, 46,
  52–53, 147–148
Credit counselors, 173
Credit unions, 140

D
Dalbar, Inc., 52
Debt, U.S. Government, 109
Deficit, U.S. Current Account, 109
Dimson, Elroy, 49
Diversification, limits of, 53–55
Dividends, importance of, 39, 67
Dow 36000, 10
Dow Jones Industrial Average,
  10, 47, 48, 124

E
Eaton Vance, 120
Emergency funds, 36–42, 46
Employee Benefits Research
  Institute, 12
Energy, savings, 154–155
Equities:
  Brazil, 53, 90
  China, 53–55, 62, 90

emerging markets, 53, 91–93
Europe, Australia and Far
  East (EAFE) Index, 93
European, 51–52
global, 55, 87–93
India, 90
individual, 66–67, 81
Japan, 52, 90–91, 123
large cap, 53
mid cap, 53
own employer's, 67–69, 81,
  126–127
price-to-earnings ratio, 59
price-to-sales ratio, 60
relation to economy, 90
Russia, 90
small cap, 56, 57, 61–62
unrealistic expectations for,
  48–53
value, 39, 57

F
401(k), 18, 35–36, 164–165, 167,
  173–174
Fannie Mae, 2, 68, 103
Federated Investors, 98–99
Fidelity Investments, 65, 167
Financial Times, 50
First Pacific Advisors, 99, 102
Four, Rule of, 159
Frazzini, Andrea, 64
Freddie Mac, 2
Fund managers:
  characteristics, 105
  performance, 65
  survey, 51
Funds, closed-end,
  118–120, 128

G
General Motors, 57
Glamour stocks, dangers of,
    66–67
Global Financial Data, Inc.,
    90, 122
Gold, 52, 73–76, 81, 108–112,
    128
Great Depression, and world
    markets, 90
Grinch, The, 151

H
Heebner, Ken, 100–102
Herzfeld, Thomas J., Advisors, 120
Home equity, 19
Home equity line of credit, 40
Home health aides, cost, 9
Hussman, John, 98–100

I
Individual retirement account
    (IRA), 18, 41, 161–168,
    173–174
Inflation, 69–73, 74, 78–80, 81,
    98, 112
Inker, Ben, 90
Insurance:
    car, 45
    cost of, 140–142
    disability, 43
    homeowners', 44
    life, 43, 166–168
    longevity, 27
    long-term care, 45
Investing, dollar cost averaging,
    121–122
iPhone, true cost of, 74, 131

J
Japan, 52, 54–55, 80, 86,
    90–91
Jaws, II, 123

K
Kellogg, Inc., 64

L
Lamont, Owed, 64
Legg Mason, 101–102
Lehman Brothers, 57, 68, 102
Lehman, Steve, 98
Leuthold Weeden Capital
    Management, 95, 97
Lipper, Inc., 63
Loyalty programs, 137,
    138, 152
Lunch:
    effective hourly wage of,
        136–137
    true cost of, 135–137
Lynch, Peter, *One Up On Wall
    Street*, 65

M
Margin debt, 40–41
Market timing, 58–61,
    120–123
Marketwatch, 104
Markowitz, Harry, 53–54
Marsh, Paul, 49
Meissner, Dana, 98
Merger Fund, The, 100
Merrill Lynch, 52, 57
Miller, Bill, 101–103
Montier, James, 66
Morningstar, Inc., 63, 104

Mortgages, paying off, 19
Munger, Charlie, 152
Mutual funds:
    absolute return, 96
    asset allocation, 94–66
    benchmarks, 61
    covered calls, 106–107
    fees, 88, 100
    flexible, 93–105, 128
    inability to hold cash, 58
    index, 88
    long-short, 95–100
    market neutral, 96
    maverick, 95, 100–103
    style boxes, 61–63
    total return, 96

N
NASDAQ, 10
National Association of
    Consumer Bankruptcy
    Attorneys, 173
National Foundation for Credit
    Counseling, 173
Netflix, Inc., 144
Nuveen Investments, 120
Nygren, Bill, 101

O
Oakmark Funds, 101
Options, put, 126–127

P
Pets.com, 10
Platinum, 75, 111
Podcasts, 145
Polaroid, 57, 68
Preferred stock, 2

R
Rallies, bear market, 122–123
Real estate, 10, 50–51, 76–80
    homestead exemption, 174
    protecting from creditors,
      174–175
    tenancy by entirety, 174–175
Realtors, National Association
    of, 79
Restaurant meals, true
    costs of, 151
Retail investors:
    chasing performance,
      63–64, 81
    poor returns of, 52
Retirement:
    costs, 8–9, 23–24
    income, 12–16
    savings, 9, 20–22
Returns, real, 10, 14–16, 20–22,
    49, 52–53, 69–72, 78–80,
    84–87, 98, 130–132
Reuters, 104
Reverse mortgage, 19
Risk, and investing, 19–20,
    55–58, 81
Rodriguez, Bob, 101–102
Romick, Steven, 98

S
Savings:
    crisis, 9–13, 19
    online, 143
Schwab, Charles, 167
Schwed, Fred Jr., *Where
    Are the Customers' Yachts?*, 56,
    126
Seeking Alpha, 104

Shiller, Robert, 61
Siegel, Jeremy, *Stocks for the Long Run*, 48
Slater, Jim, dire warning by, 124
Smith, Edgar Lawrence, *Common Stocks as Long-Term Investments*, 49
Social Security, 7, 13–15, 24–28, 177
Standard & Poor's 500, 2, 106
Staunton, Mike, 49

T
Tax loss harvesting, 171–173
Tax shelters, 161–171
Tax shelters, self-employed, 168
Tax, refunds, 34
Technology bubble, 10, 50, 62, 63–64
Telephones, cost, 145
TheStreet.com, 104
Thousand, Rule of, 159
Time, value of, 159
Twenty, Rule of, 15

U
Unemployment, 37
Union League Club, New York, 124

V
Vacation homes, 157–158
Vanguard, 95, 167
Voice over Internet Protocol (VoIP), 146

W
Waddell & Reed, 97
Waldfogel, Joel, and Christmas, 149
Wall Street Journal, 104
Washington Mutual, bankruptcy, 68
Whitman, Marty, 101
Wilde, Oscar, 100
Withholding tax, W4, 35

Y
Yahoo!, 10
Yahoo! Finance, 104

Z
Zweig, Jason, 49